CARL VICTOR BURGER was born in 1888 in East Tennessee. His grandfather was a fur trader, his own father a banker, but Carl resolved to be an artist. From his early boyhood he drew pictures of the birds and animals he saw in the Smoky Mountains, and of the fish he caught.

He attended Stanford University, was graduated from Cornell University in 1912, and went immediately to work as a newspaper cartoonist in Boston. For a brief period he taught painting at Northwestern University, and during the First World War he served as a captain of infantry in France. After the war he worked as an art director for various advertising agencies in New York.

Only a "Sunday painter" at the time, he resolved in 1930 to become a full-time freelance artist. During the next thirty-seven years he illustrated hundreds of advertisements, stories, and books; among the latter were *Old Yeller* by Fred Gipson, *The Incredible Journey* by Sheila Burnford, and *Little Rascal* by Sterling North.

He did not begin writing books himself until he was seventy-two. *All About Fish* was followed by five more titles, of which *Beaver Skins and Mountain Men* is the last. Shortly after completing the manuscript and preparing sketches for the illustrations, he died. For the most part it is his rough sketches which illustrate this book; only a few are finished work, including an exquisite drawing of the beaver skull (Chapter One), completed a few days before his death.

BEAVER SKINS
AND MOUNTAIN MEN

BEAVER SKINS AND

MOUNTAIN MEN

The importance of the beaver in the discovery, exploration, and settlement of the
North American continent

written and illustrated by
CARL BURGER

E. P. DUTTON & CO., INC. New York

Library of Congress Catalog Card Number: 68–24720

Maps by John W. Bierhorst

First Edition

C51675/76

ACKNOWLEDGMENTS

Had he lived, my father would, I am sure, have wanted to express his gratitude to various people whose special knowledge he solicited during the preparation of this book. I know personally of only two, Janet Dakin and Shepard Rifkin. These I thank in his behalf, being aware that there were others, and hoping they will understand and forgive the omission of their names.

—Knox Burger

CONTENTS

AUTHOR'S FOREWORD   11

I.   THE BEAVER

      King of the Rodents   13
      Regional Planner   19
      Inspirer of Legends   21

II.   THE LURE OF THE PELT

      Salted Cod and Other Treasure   24
      Samuel de Champlain, Father of New France   30
      Exploration and Commerce   35
      The French Go West   39
      The Great River   48
      The Sieur de La Salle   50
      Down the Mississippi and Toward the
          Western Sea   57

III. GENTLEMEN ADVENTURERS

      The Great Company   64
      The Scots Move In   71
      The Nor'westers   78
      Grand Portage   87
      The Daily Life of a Wintering Partner   90

8   CONTENTS

IV.   UP THE MISSOURI AND ACROSS THE
      ROCKIES
            Revolution and Real Estate Deal   105
            Adventure of the Two Captains   109
            Colter's Hell   115
            Astoria   119
            March of the Mountain Men   127
            A Trapper's Year   135
            Rendezvous   145
            From the Mountains to the Sea   152

V.   SUNSET OF THE MOUNTAIN MEN
            End of the Golden Harvest   167
            The Taming of the Wild Men   172
            A New Lease on Life   177

      BIBLIOGRAPHY   182

      INDEX   185

ILLUSTRATIONS AND MAPS

ILLUSTRATIONS

Beaver gnawing	frontispiece
Beavers building a lodge	15
Cross-section through beaver lodge, pond and dam	16–17
Cross-section of a beaver lodge through ice and snow	18
Beaver skull and feet	20
Beaver hat styles	26
Champlain's first battle against the Iroquois	34
Samuel de Champlain	39
Coureurs de bois	46
Hudson's Bay Company trading house	66
Voyageurs	72
Alexander Mackenzie	84
Fort Laramie	120
Mountain men hiding from Indians	134
Setting a beaver trap	136
Jim Bridger	139
Summer rendezvous	148
Settler plowing	161
Trapper with emigrants	174

MAPS

The Great Lakes and Mississippi Valley, showing explorations of Marquette, Jolliet and La Salle   56

French Canada, Hudson Bay and the Northwest   98–99

West of the Mississippi, showing the Lewis and Clark Expedition with an insert showing rendezvous sites in the Green River area   128–129

AUTHOR'S FOREWORD

THE AMERICAN BEAVER, A QUIET, UNAGGRESSIVE little animal interested only in minding its own business, has nevertheless played an important part in influencing the destiny of nations. From the earliest French occupation of Canada up to the mid-nineteenth century, the wealth to be gained from the collection of its rich fur sparked the westward march of civilization across North America to the shores of the Pacific. This book tells the story of the role played by the beaver and its enemies in the progress of that march.

When Europeans first became aware of new lands across the Atlantic, North America was a vast wilderness sparsely occupied by primitive peoples and wild beasts. For many years, only the eastern edge of the continent was charted and inhabited. How far it extended westward was a mystery to be solved only after some three centuries of exploration.

France, Spain, England, and the United States, each driven by quite different motives, were the nations that took part in the solution of this mystery.

At the end of the sixteenth century, France found herself impoverished by fruitless civil and foreign wars. The coffers of her treasury were all but empty when a way to new prosperity appeared. French fishermen from the ports of Normandy and Brittany began to bring as a sideline rich cargoes of fur from the New World. Beaver pelts, in great demand for the manufacture of hats and the decoration of clothing, would remake the fortunes of

France! For many years beaver fur was the sole commercial return from the colony of Canada, and the quest for fresh trapping grounds led its inhabitants ever to the west.

When Spain began her occupation of the Caribbean Islands, she had at last freed herself of domination by the Moors from North Africa, who had long occupied much of her country. Impoverished by the bitter struggle, she was in dire need of treasure. Gold was the remedy that would cure her ills, and her idle soldiers, thirsting for new adventures, were more than ready to seek it. This was the compelling motive of the Spaniards in exploring the newly found continent. Beaver pelts were no lure for the conquistadores, and their exploits will have little part in this story.

With the exception of the men of the Hudson's Bay Company, the English were interested primarily in establishing colonies in North America. British emigrants crossed the Atlantic to find new homes, and in the main were not interested in ranging westward beyond the Appalachians. This is not to say that there were no restless souls among them, but it was not until the English colonies had broken their ties with the mother country that the citizens of the new American republic began to look enviously toward the vast prairies beyond the Mississippi. The American surge to the Pacific was led by fur trappers, the "mountain men," who followed the beaver up the Missouri, across the Rocky Mountains, and to the western ocean.

—*C. B.*

I

THE BEAVER

King of the Rodents

TEN THOUSAND YEARS AGO THERE LIVED, ALONG with the mastodon, giant bison, and saber-toothed tiger, an animal that scientists call *Castoroides*. Its fossil remains have been found in many parts of subarctic and temperate North America. Heavier than a black bear, weighing perhaps four hundred to five hundred pounds, it measured more than seven feet from tip of nose to base of tail. A front tooth eleven-and-one-half inches long has been unearthed in Ohio. *Castoroides* was the earliest known ancestor of our modern beavers and, except in size, looked very much like them.

When the great glaciers of the Ice Age came down from the north to cover a large part of the continent, most of the gigantic beasts of that time disappeared, never to be seen again. Changes in climate, brought about by the tremendous blanket of ice, so altered their world that they could not live. But *Castoroides* somehow managed to survive through the ages, changing little in appearance, but decreasing in size. Its descendant, the modern beaver, one tenth as large, is nevertheless the world's second largest rodent. Only the capybara, a South American rodent, is larger.

The beaver is a member of the class of the animal kingdom known as mammals, those animals that suckle their young. Some of the other classes are insects, birds, and reptiles. Mammals, as all the other classes, are divided into orders, one of which is the order of rodents—the gnawing animals, such as mice, squirrels, beavers, and woodchucks. An order is made up of families, each containing one or many species. One family of the order of rodents is named

Castoridae. It contains only two species, the American beaver and the Eurasian beaver. Their scientific names are *Castor canadensis* and *Castor fiber*. According to an ancient Greek myth, Castor and his twin brother, Pollux, were the sons of Leda, and were fathered by Zeus in the form of a swan. Why the beaver family was named after one of these curiously sired twins is a mystery, but so it is called by scientists.

Beavers are strict vegetarians. They eat many kinds of grass and roots, as well as water-growing plants. But the staple diet, especially in winter, is the soft bark of such trees as birch, willow, and cottonwood. Three pounds of bark make a hearty meal for one diner, who gnaws it from a limb much as a man eats corn on the cob. But the beaver does it with greater neatness. Beavers fell trees in order to feed on the fresh bark, and to furnish logs and branches for building their dams and lodges.

The young spend their first summer and winter with the old folks. During their second spring, the parents drive them from the lodge to make room for newly born kits. The homeless young ones mature at about three years, and the male begins to search for a mate. When he finds one, the pair set out to select a site for building their own home, either in another part of the parental stream or in a nearby one. Their alliance is believed to last through life, which may be as long as sixteen years.

Having found a site to suit their fancy, usually on a small stream, the young couple builds a dam. If the water has only a gentle current, the dam is built straight across. In swifter currents it curves upstream, to give it stronger resistance to the pressure of the water.

Construction is begun with medium-sized tree limbs, and smaller ones are gradually added. The base logs are planted so they point upstream, with the larger ends anchored to the bottom with stones. Dams are long or short, depending on local conditions. One has been measured that was more than two thousand feet across. In the pool that forms above the dam, a dome-shaped lodge is built of small logs, mud, and rocks. Though the young pair has had no previous experience in building a house, they seem to know how to

Three pounds of soft bark from trees such as birch, willow and cottonwood make a hearty meal for one beaver.

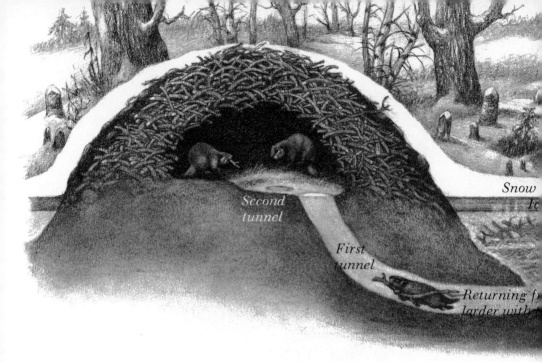

Snow

Ic

Second
tunnel

First
tunnel

Returning f
larder with

Cross-section through beaver lodge, pond and dam. The beaver usually builds a dam on a small stream. If the water has a gentle current, the dam is built straight across. In swifter currents, the dam curves upstream to give it stronger resistance to the pressure of the water.

go about it. "Working like beavers," mostly at night, they soon have the new home ready for moving in. There is no outside door. To get inside, the occupants must swim underwater to the entrance of a tunnel that leads through the foundation of the lodge to the living quarters. There is usually a second tunnel with an outlet ashore. The interior living room and nursery, its floor above water level, is carpeted with dry grass and chips, the roof above it thin enough at the top to allow some ventilation. Stones are carried from the pond's shore or bottom and plastered with mud on the outside of the lodge.

In winter, when the family is constantly at home, the walls freeze hard, and not even a bear can dig through them. The pond may freeze over, but the dam has been built high enough to assure a good depth of unfrozen water beneath the surface ice, so the occupants can swim about freely under it.

A beaver can go without breathing for about six minutes, but
that may not always be time enough to finish whatever underwater business it has in hand. If an ice sheet has sealed the pond,
there is no possibility of its rising to the surface to breathe, but it
knows how to get a supply of fresh air anyway. At one blast it
empties its lungs of all stale air, which rises to form a bubble
resting against the undersurface of the ice. Contact with the ice
chemically purifies the stale air at once. The beaver can then stick
its nose into the bubble and breathe in the purified air again. It can
do this trick over and over if it wants to prolong its underwater
stay.

On the bottom of the pond near the lodge, the provident house-
holders store enough bark-covered tree limbs to keep themselves
well fed through the winter. A quick lunch can always be had by
diving through the floor entrance to the larder below.

There in their snug living quarters the members of the family
sit through the long winter, high and dry, safe from all enemies
except man, timing their domestic affairs so that two to eight kits,

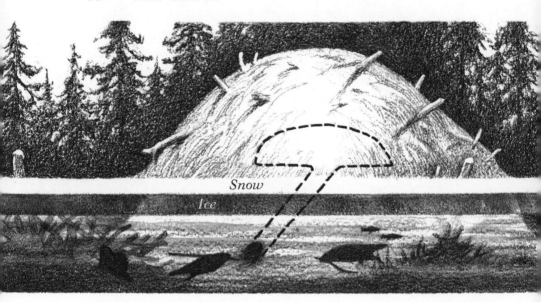

Cross-section of a beaver lodge through ice and snow. The beaver and his family are snug throughout the long winter, safe from all enemies except man. Two to eight kits, having been born at the end of winter, should be ready to venture from the lodge when spring comes.

born near the end of winter, will be ready to venture from the lodge when spring comes. Theirs is a well-ordered existence.

All rodents have long, chisel-like front teeth, but the beaver is the boss chiseler of them all. Its four curved incisors are wonderful tools for felling trees. Driven by the leverage of powerful jaws, they can fell a four-inch sapling in twenty minutes, and they sometimes cut through trunks as thick as a foot and a half. In action, the cutting ends of the two upper incisors rub against the two lower, keeping them all ground to a razor-sharp edge. As this constant honing wears down the cutting ends, the teeth grow out from their sockets in the jaws, maintaining a constant length no matter how much they may be honed.

The Eurasian beaver was once common in the northern parts of Europe and Asia, but had become extremely scarce at the time of the discovery of the New World. This species is now practically extinct. The American beaver formerly ranged from Alaska and northern Canada southward to the Gulf of Mexico, and from the Atlantic Seaboard to the Pacific Coast. It was common over all this great area with the exception of Florida and some desert regions of the Southwest. During the latter part of the nineteenth century, the beaver population was sadly depleted, and the species was in great danger of extinction. It fell to its lowest level about 1900.

The chief destroyer was man. The beaver's moated castle protects it so perfectly that it has few other enemies to fear. The otter, a very fast swimmer, can sometimes overtake it. If this meat-eating enemy catches it in the water, the peaceable, nonfighting rodent has little chance. In the water it can outswim almost any other natural enemy and retreat into the lodge, where it is safe. But the beaver is no match for the wily fur trapper. The great commercial value of its pelt led to vicious overtrapping when human enemies began to spread over areas that had been wilderness since the beginning of time. Small streams were soon cleaned out completely, and larger ones later suffered the same fate. Finally all beaver colonies were stripped from entire river systems.

The species had almost disappeared before any steps were taken to save it. Then various states began to enact laws limiting the catch, and finally to outlaw beaver-trapping altogether. State game departments tried live-trapping a few pairs from surviving colonies and transferring them to areas where local colonies had disappeared. Completely protected by law, these transplanted animals increased their numbers and spread widely. The restocking of trapped-out streams has continued steadily. With improved traps to capture the animals without injury and with airplanes to carry them quickly to new homes, it would appear that the beaver has been rescued from extinction and is making a successful comeback.

Regional Planner

The beaver is nature's outstanding hydraulic engineer. The energies of its whole life are devoted to shaping its homesite to meet its needs. It is a creature of the water, a past master of that element. Lacking the defensive protection afforded most animals by such things as speed, hooves, tusks, or horns, the beaver protects itself by building a well-nigh enemy-proof castle. On land it is slow and clumsy, and would be an easy prey for enemies if it were not clever enough to stay within easy reach of its watery sanctuary.

Trees along the pond's banks are the first to be felled. Then they are cut into sections and floated to the dam or lodge site, with the beaver swimming alongside holding by its teeth to a projecting limb, much as a tugboat eases a ship into its dock. When at length all suitable trees near the pond's banks are consumed, the clever engineers dig canals through which trees cut at a greater distance from the bank can be floated to the pond. Or they may build a second dam a short distance upstream to reach a fresh supply of timber. When, after living for years in the same lodge, a family has used all the food trees within reach, it abandons the old home and builds a new one at another location.

This animal is well equipped for the life it leads. In both the ears and nostrils are valves which, when closed, keep out all water. The eyes are protected by transparent membranes that serve as built-in diving goggles. Two folds of skin, just behind the gnawing

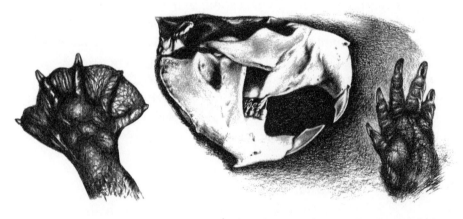

In the center, the beaver skull showing cutting teeth. On the left, the large webbed hind foot. On the right, the small and efficient front foot.

teeth, can be drawn tightly together, making it possible to gnaw while submerged without getting a mouthful of water. The large hind feet are webbed for swimming, and the smaller unwebbed front feet are almost as efficient as human hands. The nail of the second toe of each hind foot is split into two parts to form a serviceable comb, which is a handy and much used tool for grooming the fur.

A unique feature of beaver anatomy is the tail, which is shaped like the blade of a canoe paddle and covered with scales. It is used as a rudder in swimming and serves as a staunch rear prop when its owner sits on hindquarters felling a tree. It is not used as a sledge for carrying house-building material, though many old engravings show it being used in that way. Mud and rocks are carried by being held against the breast by the forefeet. The fact that the beaver spends much of its time in the water and has scales on its tail once led certain church authorities to rule that it was not a mammal but a fish, and so could be lawfully eaten during Lent and on holy days. When surprised by an intruder, a swimming beaver slaps its tail on the surface of the water with a resounding crack, a signal to warn its fellows that danger threatens. This startling sound, when heard in the wilderness, carries for half a mile or more and may be repeated by other beavers that are far away.

Inspirer of Legends

The Indians of early American history held the beaver in great respect, as is shown by many of their legends and religious myths. In some tribes this esteem approached veneration.

One legend, prominent in the lore of the Cherokees and several other tribes, accounts for the creation of the earth in this novel fashion: Manitou, the creator, having made a water-covered world inhabited by gigantic beavers, soon realized that there must also be accommodation for the land-living animals whose creation he had in mind. Puzzled as to how this could be brought about, he sought advice of the beavers. With their usual sagacity and industry, the obliging animals dived to the bottom of the ocean and brought up vast quantities of mud and stones. Being so clever at building their own lodges, they easily fashioned from this material the continents with their plains, mountains, and valleys.

Another legend, common among eastern tribes, accounts for the creation of man in this way : All ancient beavers possessed the gift of language. But some of the tough ones used such wicked words that Manitou in disgust changed them into men. This might be taken as a bit of primitive satire.

Among the Hidatsas, who lived far up the Missouri, a beaver bone was placed in the sacred medicine lodge along with other magic objects. This was a gesture of thanks to all the beavers that had died to furnish meat for Hidatsa feasts. It was hoped that this grateful recognition would also influence living beavers to be less shy and wily in avoiding hunters.

The Chippewas occasionally reported to French trappers the sighting of giant beavers in Lake Superior. An especially huge one had been changed by some powerful wizard into an island thirty miles long. One of the exploits of Manabozho, an Indian Paul Bunyan, was the pursuit of a monstrous beaver through Lakes Superior and Huron into the Ottawa River. Here he finally overtook the monster, seized it, and smashed its head against a great boulder. The violent contact left a huge bloody splash on the rock, ever afterward held in awe by local Indians. It may be guessed that French trappers to whom this remarkable landmark was pointed out received the story with some skepticism. They may even have guessed that the red boulder was the inspiration of the tale, rather than the result of the exploit.

The Algonquin tribes along the St. Lawrence River believed that thunder was the sound made by Quahbeet, their beaver father, as he slapped the surface of a lake with his tail. Other tribes not of the Algonquin nation also considered the beaver their tribal ancestor.

The five nations of the powerful Iroquois Confederacy, one of the few examples of successful cooperation between tribes of American Indians, were closely bound together by various clans common to all the five nations. One of these was called the beaver clan, and its members were known as the beaver people. The Crows, who lived in present-day Montana, believed that men, after death, came back to earth in the form of beavers. To a member of this tribe, any beaver might be a near relative or close friend.

The Flatheads, another western tribe, held that beavers were a race of men who had angered the Great Spirit, and for their sins had been changed into animals sentenced to perpetual hard labor.

Indians relished beaver meat. It was a part of their regular diet, but was used especially for ceremonial occasions, such as a feast to honor visiting friends or to celebrate a victory. After enough beavers for a feast had been caught and cleaned, the carcasses were impaled on skewers and roasted in their skins. The liver and tail were considered the choice cuts. Only a few animals were captured from any one beaver pond, and never from one near the village where the feast was to be held. The nearby beavers were considered friends and were not to be disturbed. The feasters evidently felt some qualms at eating an animal so closely identified with themselves. Bones and scraps left over after a beaver feast were carefully gathered into baskets and sunk in deep water, where they could not be dishonored by wolves and other scavengers.

II

THE LURE OF THE PELT

Salted Cod and Other Treasure

IN THE LATE SUMMER OF 1534, A SMALL CARAVEL made her way through the narrow Strait of Belle Isle, which leads from the Atlantic into the Gulf of St. Lawrence. Her sails and rigging showed the wear of a long and stormy voyage. She had weighed anchor late in April at the ancient port of St.-Malo on the western coast of France. On her deck, gazing at the forbidding shores of Newfoundland and Labrador on either side, stood her stocky, rough-hewn captain, Jacques Cartier, born forty years before of a family of hardy Breton mariners.

Cartier's ship had been sent out by Philippe de Brion Chabot, French admiral and boon companion of Francis I, the king. Chabot's object was twofold. He burned with zeal to save the lost souls of the infidels of the New World by converting them to the Roman Catholic Church, recently abandoned by the followers of Luther and the Reformers. Perhaps more zealously, he burned to discover a new sea route to the pearls and spices of the East Indies.

The only known route from Europe to the fabulous riches of the Orient had always been an interminable voyage around the southern tip of Africa and eastward across the tremendous reaches of the Indian Ocean. Columbus, on the novel theory that the world was round, had sailed westward from Spain forty-two years before Cartier's voyage. Columbus had believed that he could reach China by this route, and so he could have if the two Americas had not barred the way.

Ever since the first voyage of Columbus, mariners had been

convinced that a waterway leading to China must cut somewhere across the newly discovered continent of North America, and the search for such a passage was long the lodestone that drew adventurers westward. Belief in this will-o'-the-wisp, the so-called Northwest Passage, was not finally laid to rest until the end of the eighteenth century, when land exploration had proved that no such waterway existed short of the frozen Arctic.

Sailing through the Strait of Belle Isle, Cartier found that it led into a great gulf, now called the Gulf of St. Lawrence, which he spent many weeks in exploring. As winter came on, he turned his prow eastward and made his way back across the Atlantic. In spite of the meager results of this voyage, Cartier returned to St.-Malo convinced that the gulf he had explored was the entrance to a water route across North America leading to the western sea. Later he was to learn better. The only plunder he carried home was two young Indians, dressed in beaver fur, whom he had lured aboard his ship.

Jacques Cartier was by no means the first European who had sailed these cold northern waters, but he was the first whose voyage enjoyed royal support and gained wide public attention. For many years before him, adventurous fishermen from the ports of France, Spain, and Portugal had crossed the Atlantic to ply their trade in the shallow seas off the island of Newfoundland.

Here the waters teemed with tremendous schools of codfish, so abundant that they sometimes impeded the progress of their small ships. The cod was in great demand in the markets of Europe, for its flesh, when salted and dried, kept fresh for a long time and could be carried to distant markets for use during Lent and holy days. Old records show that in 1517 fifty Spanish, French, and Portuguese vessels were present on the Newfoundland Banks at the same time, while in August of 1527, in the Newfoundland harbor of St. John's, there were "eleven saile of Normans, and one of Brittainy and two Portugall Barkes, and all a-fishing."

Some of these bold mariners had even ventured westward from Newfoundland across the Gulf of St. Lawrence and sailed up the great St. Lawrence River as far as the mouth of the Saguenay.

French
17th Century

Stovepipe
19th Century

Cavalier
English

Milita
18th Centu

Holland
17th Century

Wellington
English

Naval
Cocked
Hat

French
18th Century

French
17th Century

Beaver hat styles in vogue—17th, 18th and 19th centuries. Beaver pelt was the best material for making felt and was used in the huge plumed hats worn by European gentlemen.

Here they traded cheap baubles for the beaver robes worn by the inhabitants of an Indian village called Tadoussac. This trade in furs came more and more to interest French fishermen. The Indians valued beaver pelts only as winter clothing and bed robes, but the fur sold at a handsome price in France. This was the best material for making felt, and was used in great quantity for the manufacture of the huge plumed hats worn by European gentlemen.

Felt is not a woven material like most other cloth. An animal's fur is of two types—the guard hair, long and coarse, and the underhair, much shorter and finer. To make felt, the guard hair is trimmed off and the soft underhair is made into a smooth, tough material by being matted under heat and pressure. It can be molded into any desired shape. Beaver pelts make the best of all felt, because the underhairs are covered with tiny barbs, which make them mat, or cling closely together, when pressed.

The Indians would gladly trade a prime beaver pelt for a few glass beads, brass buttons, or fishhooks, and a cargo of furs was far more valuable than a load of salted cod. Especially valued for making felt were the pelts that had been worn for some time as garments by the highly odorous Indians, for the guard hairs then loosened and dropped out. The only difficulty was that not enough beaver pelts were available to make them the sole object of a voyage—unless the Indians could be persuaded to catch more beavers. So salt cod necessarily retained first place as the merchandise sought by these early adventurers.

The shrewd fishermen jealously guarded as a trade secret the location of their treasure trove, and no one else knew where they found the riches they brought home. Returned sailors would say only that they had been to Bacalaos, a name derived from the Basque word for "codfish."

In the spring of the year following his first voyage, Cartier again set sail for Bacalaos, resolved to explore further his fancied Northwest Passage. He commanded three vessels, had a few adventurous nobles as aides, and a motley crew recruited along the waterfront of St.-Malo.

After going through the Strait of Belle Isle, the fleet sailed some eight hundred miles up the St. Lawrence and anchored off a lofty headland, grim and forbidding. Here Cartier led a party ashore and followed friendly Indian guides up a rocky path to the top of the cliff, where they found a cluster of rude bark huts. This was the seat of a chieftain named Donnacona, "the king of this domain," as Cartier put it. The straggling village was called Stadacona by its inhabitants. These same heights were to be scaled long afterward by an English army to capture Quebec.

At Stadacona, Cartier learned that a more important town called Hochelaga was located farther up the river, and he set out with his smallest ship to find it. At Hochelaga the party was met by a crowd of excited Indians who led them through the forest to a large village at the foot of a mountain. Cartier named the place Montreal, Royal Mountain. After a feast of wild game, which the Frenchmen relished, and much oratory, which they did not understand, they bade their hosts farewell at the waterfront and went back down the river. They had visited Stadacona and Hochelaga, Quebec and Montreal, then as now the chief cities of eastern Canada.

Returning to Quebec, were the men left there had built a rude log fort, the Frenchmen went into winter quarters. And a gruesome winter it was. The river froze over, great snowdrifts almost buried the fort. The three ships were threatened with starvation, and scurvy, the scourge of sailors, struck down twenty-five of the men.

When spring came at length and thawed the ships free of their icy prison, the woebegone party set sail for home. They had accumulated a small cargo of beaver skins by trading with the Indians, who were for the most part hospitable. The Frenchmen repaid their hospitality by seizing Donnacona and some of his lesser chieftains and carrying them away to France. Within a year or so all the Indians were dead.

Five years went by before Cartier again set sail for Bacalaos, which he had renamed Canada, after an Indian word meaning "town" or "village." The backer of this venture was the Sieur de Roberval, a new favorite of Francis I, who had named him viceroy. This nobleman was inspired by three worthy motives: he would found a colony, convert the natives to the Roman Church, and grow wealthy at the fur trade.

Leaving Roberval to collect a group of colonists, Cartier crossed the Atlantic, sailed up the St. Lawrence, and went ashore at Quebec. Here he set his men at building two new forts, one on the riverbank and one at the top of the cliff. Going on with a small party to explore the river, he found above Montreal wild rapids that churned the water to foam for miles. Seeing that this was surely no open route to China, the disappointed explorers rejoined their shipmates at Quebec, where the united company wintered.

After waiting in vain until spring for Roberval to appear, they abandoned their forts and started home—they had had their fill of pioneering. At the harbor of St. John's in Newfoundland they found Roberval. He had been delayed a year by unforeseen difficulties, and was now on his way to Quebec with three hundred colonists. Sick of the whole venture, Cartier ignored the commander's order to turn back, and went on his way to France. The angry viceroy was obliged to finish his voyage to Quebec without him.

The character of Roberval's colonists was hardly ideal for a group whose mission was the establishment of Christianity in a wild and trackless wilderness. Most of them were convicted criminals whom the king had empowered his viceroy to free from prison on their promise to settle permanently in Canada.

At Quebec the hardships of a Canadian winter tore the colony to shreds. The motley crowd of settlers, most of them the dregs of seacoast towns, had no experience with the forest, and their attempts at trapping beaver and trading with Indians met with no success whatsoever. Roberval proved to be a cruel commander and sentenced men and women to be hanged or exiled to the woods for petty crimes. No one knows what happened to the luckless settlement, but it is certain that it did not last for long.

After various other short-lived attempts to found colonies in Canada, France was for many years ravaged by religious wars. Huguenots and Catholics were so busy tearing at one another's throats that no official attempts were made to exploit the riches of the New World. During this time, however, the stolid French fishermen, indifferent to the religious struggle, calmly went about their business on the Newfoundland Banks and in the St. Lawrence. They came to realize that the riches harvested from the sea might be surpassed by the riches to be gathered from the forests.

Trading posts were set up on the large island of Anticosti in the Gulf of St. Lawrence. These posts attracted many Indians, who were happy to trade the spoils of their hunting for a few knives, hatchets, and glass beads. Many a ship returned to France laden with beaver pelts, worth many times the value of a cargo of codfish. Merchants in St.-Malo and other ports of western France greedily went into this new and more profitable trade, and began to finance voyages whose sole object was the collection of furs.

In 1589 Henry of Navarre, ruler of a small kingdom in the Pyrenees Mountains, brought the civil wars to an end by vanquishing his enemies and ascending the throne of France as Henry IV. Though he had been a leader of the Huguenot forces, he had no great regard for creeds or dogmas and made himself acceptable to both factions by embracing the Catholic faith. Under his wise rule, France could now lick her wounds and return to peaceful pursuits.

Samuel de Champlain, Father of New France

In 1607, Henry IV authorized the Sieur de Monts, who had already made a failure of a colony in present-day Nova Scotia, to attempt the planting of another colony in Canada. This nobleman was loaded with titles, but was short of cash. To pay expenses, he was granted a monopoly of the beaver trade for one year. He formed a company of merchants, and fitted out two ships that sailed from Honfleur in Normandy in April of 1608.

One vessel, with a cargo of goods for the Indian trade, was commanded by a merchant named Pontgravé. The other, loaded with men, arms, and supplies for the colony, was commanded by Samuel de Champlain, a romantic soldier with an unquenchable thirst for adventure.

Though a devout Catholic, he had fought through the civil wars on the side of the Huguenots and stood high in the good graces of the king. For the remainder of his life, the struggling colony in Canada was to be his first love. He is known as the "father of New France."

On arriving at Tadoussac, Champlain left Pontgravé to trade there for beaver and went up the river to Quebec. Here he built quarters for his men on the narrow beach at the base of the cliff, where they spent the bitterly cold winter. An epidemic of scurvy reduced his force of twenty-eight men to eight, and half of these were suffering from the disease.

The coming of spring brought health to the weakened party. It brought also the return of Pontgravé from a voyage home, where he had marketed the rich cargo of beaver pelts collected from the Indians at Tadoussac.

Pontgravé remained at Quebec to carry on his trading, leaving Champlain free to turn to his cherished exploration of the upper St. Lawrence. Though this was his great ambition, he could not ignore the fact that extension of the fur trade must come first. Beaver pelts were the only resource by which the colony could be made profitable to the king and enjoy the continued support of its financial backers.

At Quebec, visiting Huron Indians from far up the Ottawa River had told Champlain of the vast number of beavers to be found in the upper reaches of that stream, which flows into the St. Lawrence at Montreal. Even more tempting were stories the upriver Indians told of the many huge lakes in their country. Champlain fervently hoped these lakes would lead him to the western sea.

A way to gain the friendship and secure the fur trade of these western tribes was unexpectedly opened to him. He was invited by a Huron chief to bring his armor-clad soldiers with their deadly fire sticks to join the Hurons and their allies, the Algonquins, in a war against the Iroquois. This was the sort of adventure that appealed to Champlain. He could make friends of the tribes of the upper Ottawa, persuade them to bring furs down the river to trade at Montreal, and make himself welcome to explore their country. He immediately accepted the invitation, never suspecting what the outcome would be. This was a mere lark that would further the fortunes of the colony and redound to the glory of the king.

The Indians against whom Champlain had so lightheartedly agreed to fight were members of the League of the Five Nations, by far the most warlike and powerful of all the tribes in that part of the continent. Also they were great orators. The name by which the French called them, "Iroquois," stemmed from their custom of ending all orations with the word "*Hiro*," meaning, "I have said it." They called themselves "Hodenosaunee," "the People of the Long House."

The Iroquois lived in long, rectangular wigwams of bark, each having five fires symbolizing the five confederated nations: Mohawks, Senecas, Oneidas, Cayugas, and Onondagas. They lived in what is now central New York from the Hudson River westward to the Genesee. They were traditional enemies of Champlain's allies. The warpath the Iroquois traveled on many savage forays against their northern neighbors led from the upper Hudson River through two large lakes, and down the River Richelieu to its junction with the St. Lawrence. Iroquois war parties infested the forests to the west of Montreal, and would greatly increase the dangers of French trade and exploration in that quarter.

Champlain's Indian allies, most of whom had never seen a white man, came to Quebec late in June. They were thunderstruck at the marvels they found there: soldiers dressed in iron, the wonderful log fort and cabins, the booming of small arms and cannon. After they had been welcomed at a sumptuous feast, they bedaubed their bodies with war paint and danced themselves into a martial frenzy.

The war party set out as soon as the dance was over. Champlain, in a small sailboat with eleven of his French soldiers, was at the head of twenty-four canoes carrying sixty Indian warriors. When they reached the mouth of the Richelieu, they made their way up its stiff current, camping ashore each night. Violent rapids at length made it impossible for the sailboat to go any farther, and Champlain was forced to order it back to Quebec with all but two of his French soldiers, with whom he continued in the Indian canoes. At the source of the Richelieu, they entered the long, narrow body of water now called Lake Champlain. Here they were in enemy country and traveled only at night, lying concealed in the forest during the day.

One evening they saw a fleet of Iroquois canoes rounding a point of land ahead of them. Both parties set up a defiant yell, and the Iroquois went ashore, where they began cutting trees to make a rough breastwork. The Hurons and Algonquins kept to their canoes. All through the night both sides worked themselves into a passion of rage by shouting insults at one another, while the three Frenchmen kept themselves hidden under robes in the bottom of the boats.

When daylight came, the attackers landed and advanced through the woods. As they neared the makeshift breastwork, they halted and opened ranks to allow their French champions to march to the front. The bold approach of these three ironclad warriors terrified the Iroquois. These could not be men! They must be gods fallen from the sky to come to the aid of the hated enemy.

Champlain's own narrative tells the story of what followed:

When I saw them getting ready to shoot their arrows at us, I leveled my harquebus, which I had loaded with four balls, and aimed straight at one of the three chiefs. The shot brought down two and wounded another. On this our Indians set up such a yelling that one could not have heard a thunderclap, and all the while the arrows flew thick on both sides. The Iroquois were greatly astonished and frightened to see two of their men killed so quickly, in spite of their arrow-proof reed armor. As I was reloading, one of my companions fired a shot from the woods, which so increased their astonishment that, seeing their chiefs dead, they abandoned the field and fled into the depths of the forest.

The allies pursued the terrified enemy, captured or killed many, and took all their abandoned canoes and equipment. It was an overwhelming victory.

This affair was typical of most Indian wars, which were an endless succession of skirmishes that almost never led to any real result. It is important to our story only because it was the first fight in which Frenchmen took part on the side of one Indian nation against another. It made the powerful Iroquois Confederacy lasting enemies of the French, and led to a long series of murderous raids which at times came near to wrecking the colony.

The bitter animosity of the Iroquois prevented southern extension of the French fur trade, and forced it to expand westward up the Ottawa River into Lake Huron, through the other Great Lakes, and eventually down the Mississippi. This, among other events, resulted in the claim of France to all the central interior of North

In this, Champlain's first battle against the Iroquois, many of the enemy were either captured or killed.

America. But Champlain's alliance with the enemies of the Iroquois, in this battle and later ones, was the foundation of a long-lasting enmity that vitally influenced the future of Canada.

Shortly after Champlain's decisive part in this battle, he and Pontgravé went to France to confer with their patron, the Sieur de Monts, whose fur trade monopoly had been revoked. They determined to go on with their plans in spite of this. On Champlain's return to Quebec, he found that independent traders had flocked to the St. Lawrence, where they were busily filling their ships with fur. Now that Monts no longer held a monopoly, this stiff competition was entirely lawful. So Champlain determined to explore the possibilities for beaver-trapping up the Ottawa in the virgin country of his friends, the Hurons and Algonquins. There, they told him, beavers were plentiful.

His first concern was to set up a trading post at Montreal to which the upriver tribes could bring, down the Ottawa, the furs they had promised to collect. This he believed would strangle the business of independent traders farther down the St. Lawrence.

But the competition promptly moved up to Montreal, where many small traders soon assembled, greedily awaiting the arrival from upriver of the first flotilla of fur-laden canoes. When at length they came dancing down the rapids, they were greeted by such a blast of firearms that the visitors hardly dared come ashore. The volley was meant as a hearty welcome, but the Indians were sure that all these wild men meant to murder them and steal their furs. Their fears were set at rest by Champlain, their pelts were traded for kettles, knives, brandy, and baubles, and they went happily back up the river to their villages.

This was the first of a long series of Montreal trading fairs. They grew in importance, picturesqueness, and violence as the years went by, and became the most fantastic feature of the Canadian fur trade.

Exploration and Commerce

When Champlain returned to Montreal in May of 1615 from another voyage to France, he was accompanied by four priests, members of the Recollets, a branch of the Franciscan Order. Their mission was to be the conversion of the Indians. A fixed policy had been adopted by Champlain and Pontgravé. All the tribes menaced by the Iroquois were to be persuaded to live at peace with one another, and to combine under French leadership against the common enemy.

With French priests to baptize them, French soldiers to help them fight, and French trading posts where they could exchange their beaver skins for manufactured goods, they would become completely dependent on the colony. The three instruments of this desired result, priests, soldiers, and traders, would all work to encourage the Indians to supply more pelts, the "soft gold" of New France.

At a council of Algonquins and Hurons at Montreal, a grand alliance against the Iroquois was formed. The Indians agreed to assemble an army of warriors at the Huron towns, where Champlain promised to join them with his soldiers. After a hurried trip to Quebec, he set out up the Ottawa with Étienne Brulé, his lieutenant and interpreter, one other Frenchman, and a few Indians. Twelve well-armed soldiers had already left Montreal to await him at the Huron towns.

The tremendous swarms of mosquitoes proved to be a greater torture than all other challenges of the wild river. A Recollet priest, following the same route a few years later, feelingly described the miseries he suffered. "These little beasts not only persecute you all day," he wrote, "but at night they get into your eyes and mouth, crawl under your clothes and stick their stings through them, and make such a noise that it distracts your attention and prevents you from saying your prayers."

The insect-tortured travelers went far up the river, turned west to cross Lake Nipissing, and at last gazed in awe over the vast reaches of Lake Huron, the Sweetwater Sea of the Hurons. The prosperous nation that lived here among their rudely cultivated fields numbered some thirty thousand people. Though they were blood relations of the Iroquois, the two peoples were chronically at war with one another.

As they had promised, the allied tribes were assembling at the Huron towns for a war against their powerful foe, and joyfully welcomed Champlain as the hero who would lead them to victory. But their champion would reap little glory from this campaign.

The undisciplined horde crossed Lake Ontario and made its way to a fortified Iroquois town a few miles south of Lake Oneida in today's New York. A planned surprise assault was spoiled by the impatience of a few young warriors, who rushed ahead to attack a group of women working in the fields. This alerted the enemy and the assault failed. After a few days of shouting insults and shooting arrows aimlessly at the palisade surrounding the village, the fierce invaders gave up and went home. Champlain was seriously wounded in the fight and had to be carried all the way back.

The great alliance fell apart. Champlain's carefully organized attempt to crush the Iroquois had failed, though he was in no way responsible, and he had sustained a great loss of prestige. He spent the winter in the lodge of a Huron chief, recovering from his wounds, making friends among the neighboring villages, and losing no opportunity to tell the people of the glories of Montreal and the wonderful things to be exchanged for their beaver skins. After his return to Quebec in the spring, he roamed the forests no more. He was now temporal head of the colony, and the pressing duties of that office obliged him to give up the adventure he loved.

After several changes of overlords in France, the Duc de Montréal was named viceroy of Canada. He revoked all previous monopolies, and granted the fur trade to two Huguenot brothers, William and Emery de Caen. The former holders refused to give up their monopolies, and the two factions, after much bickering, settled their quarrel by combining forces.

On the river the Huguenot sailors of the Caen brothers held daily religious services aboard their ships, and greatly scandalized the devout Catholics ashore by their lusty singing of Calvinist hymns. This formidable danger to the spiritual welfare of the colony was averted by an order forbidding the heretical sailors to sing, but allowing them to pray. Since prayers could not be heard by those ashore, the Caens, in spite of their heresy, prospered mightily. They paid shareholders in their company an annual dividend of 40 percent, and in one particularly good season shipped from Canada twenty-two thousand beaver skins.

Under the weak king, Louis XIII, Cardinal Richelieu, the chief minister, became the real ruler of France. Dissatisfied with the management of the colony in Canada, he completely reorganized it in 1627. He formed a group of one hundred shareholders to be known as the Company of New France, with himself at its head.

The investors, of whom Champlain was one, were men of substance—nobles, merchants, and wealthy citizens. They were granted a complete monopoly of the fur trade, and on their part bound themselves to send out enough permanent settlers of both sexes to swell the population of Canada to four thousand by the year 1643. All settlers were to be French and Roman Catholic. There was to be no more heresy!

In France the religious wars broke out anew. Charles I of England sent a fleet to aid the Huguenots, and also sent out a naval expedition under Captain David Kirke to seize the French possessions in North America. When Kirke's squadron appeared off Quebec, the pitifully weak garrison was in no position to put up a fight. A supply ship was long overdue, the magazine of the fort held only fifty pounds of powder, the garrison was weakened by sickness, and the people were near starvation.

Kirke took the town without resistance, and carried Champlain and his band of soldiers to England as prisoners. All the efforts of the bold adventurer who had been the heart and soul of the colony seemed to have come to an end.

But before Kirke's fleet reached home, the two warring nations had agreed to settle their differences at a peace conference. Partly through the efforts of Champlain, the terms of the treaty restored Canada to France.

An argument even more potent than the pleas of Champlain influenced the English king to renounce such a valuable prize. Due to his quarrels with Parliament, Charles was extremely short of funds. The French government still owed him half the dowry they had agreed to pay on his marriage to Henrietta Maria, a sister of Louis XIII. The English king refused to honor the terms of the treaty relating to Canada until the balance due on his queen's dowry was forthcoming. When the account was at last balanced, the impecunious English monarch pocketed the money and relinquished his loot.

Champlain returned to his cherished colony in 1633, commissioned by Richelieu to command in behalf of the Company of New France. Under the influence of Jesuit fathers, now the spiritual powers in Canada, Quebec came more and more to resemble a religious community. Champlain, an extremely devout man, supported the priests wholeheartedly, and prayers, masses, and confessions claimed much of the time of the soldiers and citizens.

From Quebec Jesuit fathers penetrated distant wildernesses,

Samuel de Champlain, who gave the best years of his life to the wise and clear-sighted service of New France.

establishing missions where they suffered discouragement, misery, and martyrdom. But always they held to the twofold purpose of converting the heathen and bringing them to a more complete dependence on the French as the only means of satisfying their growing desire for trade goods.

At last on Christmas day of 1635, Champlain, broken by many years of labor for his people, passed away, sincerely mourned by priests, soldiers, and the handful of settlers. He had given the best years of his life to the wise and clear-sighted service of New France, and the colony must now carry on under less devoted leaders.

The French Go West

From the days when Breton fishermen first traded for pelts at Anticosti Island, it had been the policy of the colonial government to encourage the Indians to collect beaver skins, cure them, and bring them to established trading posts where they could barter for the merchandise they had learned to covet.

In the early days of the trade, few Frenchmen went into the forest to trap. The natives shot the animals with bow and arrow, hunting at dusk or by moonlight from canoes, or hiding in bushes along the shore. At times they captured beavers by using snares, pits, or deadfalls. Indians relished the meat, especially the tail, but before the coming of the French they hunted beavers primarily to make clothing of the fur. They killed comparatively few, and were careful not to take too many from any one stream.

If a large quantity of meat was needed, as for a ceremonial feast, a party of hunters with dogs selected a pond, sealed off the spillway of the dam, and chopped through the walls of a lodge with axes. This drove the beavers out into their escape tunnels, some of which had outlets ashore. When a dog's barking announced that it had located a beaver in one of the under-shore tunnels, hunters blocked it off by driving long stakes into the ground. Then they dug into the tunnel, and speared the imprisoned animal or captured it with their hands.

As the French demand for pelts and their own need for trade goods mounted, Indians increased their hunting efforts. Formerly they had taken only what was needed for food and robes, but they became more and more fascinated by the luxuries offered at the trading posts: copper kettles, glass beads, mirrors, and, most fascinating of all, brandy. This was to become the most coveted luxury, ruinous to the customers and a source of never-ending trouble to the colonial authorities, who strove in vain to forbid, or at least to regulate, the traffic. The primitive Indian had only one object when brandy was available—to drink himself into a stupor as quickly as possible. In time, liquor became the scourge of all the tribes.

This increasing appetite for luxury resulted in an early scarcity of beaver in the lower reaches of the St. Lawrence. To the south of the river, the hostility of the Iroquois made trapping extremely dangerous. To the north, the lazy and improvident Montagnais tribes showed little interest in acquiring luxuries. As a result, beaver trappers were driven to seek virgin hunting grounds to the west.

We have seen how Champlain went far up the Ottawa to implant a yearning for trade goods among the Algonquins and Hurons, always urging them to bring their pelts down the river to his post at Montreal. In 1615 he sent his interpreter and fellow explorer Étienne Brulé south from Lake Huron to stir up trade.

Brulé crossed Lake Ontario, kept on going south, gained the headwaters of the Susquehanna River, and followed it to its mouth at the head of Chesapeake Bay. As he was returning from this long journey, he was captured by a band of Iroquois, who plucked part of his beard and began their usual fiendish tortures. When one of the tormentors reached for a religious medal that hung about his neck, Brulé cried, "If you touch that, you and all your race will die!"

At that moment a flash of lightning rent the sky, followed by a tremendous thunderclap. The torturers fled in terror. After this demonstration of godlike power, Brulé was held in superstitious awe by his captors, who released him and finally guided him to Montreal.

Étienne Brulé was a picturesque character. He liked Indians, loved their way of life, and was adept at learning their languages. When he was still in his teens, Champlain sent him to live for a year among the natives to the west of the Ottawa.

Brulé's job was to explore the country, encourage the tribes to hunt, and return the beaver harvest to Montreal. He dressed and painted himself like a Huron and married a Huron girl. He was constantly in the bad graces of the priests, for he set a bad example to their converts, neglecting to observe holy days, drinking heavily, and making merry with the squaws of various tribes. This was contrary to religious teaching, but it was good for business, for it made him a welcome visitor and kinsman wherever he went. Brulé's passion for exploration equaled Champlain's, and he spent much of his life roaming the wilderness.

The first French explorations to the west by Champlain and Brulé were soon followed by Jesuit priests and beaver trappers, whose wanderings acquainted them with the general geography of the Great Lakes. At the several connecting straits that join these vast inland seas were located the chief missions and trading centers. From the first, the most widely used access to the lake country was Champlain's route up the Ottawa, across Lake Nipissing, then west to Georgian Bay of Lake Huron. At the southern end of this bay, Father Jean de Brébeuf, a Jesuit, founded the mission where he struggled so long against the heathen gods of the Hurons, only to have his parishioners finally massacred by the Iroquois, and to suffer his own martyrdom by torture.

At the Sault, where the waters of Lake Superior plunged through wild rapids into Lake Huron, was the mission and trading post of Sainte Marie du Sault. This was a favorite fishing spot, where many of the Algonquin tribes assembled every spring and summer to feast on the abundant harvest of the strait. At the Sault today stands the Michigan city of Sault Ste. Marie. The demands of commerce have tamed the cataract. A canal with locks now carries great ships smoothly around the rapids whose thunder once awed the *voyageur* and forced him to shoulder his canoe for a long and wearisome portage.

The little island of Mackinac lies in the narrow strait between Lakes Huron and Michigan. This rocky islet, then called Michilimackinac, was the chief center of French fur trade in the Great Lakes country. Here was held a yearly fair, attended by many tribes of the surrounding wilderness. French trappers came out of the forests to sell their beaver skins and add their unrestrained revelry to the general pandemonium. The garrison of the fort, whose duty it was to keep order, only added to the disorder. Both officers and soldiers engaged in liquor traffic, in spite of the scandalized protests of the priests. To add to the universal debauchery, many Indian girls made the post a center for practicing their profession.

The strait connecting Lakes Erie and Huron was a much-traveled path, and its trading post, Detroit, always did a thriving business. The Niagara River, interrupted by the great falls, was a difficult passage from Erie to Ontario, and had the added disadvantage of being close to Iroquois war parties. It never ranked as a trading center with the other passages between the lakes. Less important missions and trading posts were located at the southern end of Green Bay of Lake Michigan, at La Pointe, near the western end of Lake Superior, and, as time went on, at many other places in the lake country.

From all these centers, the glory and might of France were constantly proclaimed to visiting customers by both priests and laymen. And every Indian yearned to carry his furs occasionally to Montreal, the great center of trade, where he was told that undreamed-of wonders and delights awaited him.

The annual trading fair at Montreal outshone all others in size, picturesqueness, and debauchery. Established by order of the king, its object was to discourage the colonists from going to the Indians, and to induce the Indians to come to them. No pains were spared in tempting the natives to make the long and dangerous descent of the Ottawa. As the time for the fair approached, every man of any consequence in the town prepared to reap a share of the rich harvest. All local traders, as well as merchants from Quebec and farther down the river, brought their wares and set up shop outside the palisades that were supposed to protect the town from the rowdy throng.

As the fleets of fur-laden canoes came careening down the rapids, they were met with shouts of welcome and the blasts of trumpets and firearms. The Indians landed, unloaded their bales of beaver fur, set up wigwams in an assigned area, and slung their kettles over cooking fires.

On the opening day of the fair, all assembled for a grand council. The governor, his sword across his knees, sat in majestic grandeur in his gilded chair, backed by the military, clergy, and citizenry. The motley horde of Indians, perhaps a thousand strong, seated themselves on the ground in a half circle facing the officials. Here were savages dressed in little but feathers and paint, French bushrangers tricked out more fantastically than the savages, priests in their somber robes, officers in dress uniform complete with plumed hats, and soldiers in armor, as well as merchants and habitants wearing their best clothes. The entire day was given over to welcoming speeches by the governor and his lieutenants, interminable orations by important chieftains, and ceremonial pipe-smoking.

Trading began briskly next morning and went into full swing as the day wore on. In spite of the efforts of priests and officials, the sale of brandy could not be suppressed, and as the fiery liquor began to take effect the party often got out of hand. It wound up in an orgy of drunken frenzy, with stark naked Indians reeling through the streets of the town brandishing their weapons, and the more staid citizens barricading themselves inside their houses. Not until the last canoe had breasted the rapids for the homeward voyage could the exhausted merchants take time to reckon their gains. They were considerable.

A profit of at least 50 percent was usual on staples such as kettles and blankets, while for luxuries such as beads and brandy, gains of several hundred percent were common. With the recklessness induced by strong drink, the customer was inclined to throw his beaver skins on the counter and take whatever was offered in return.

Baron Lahontan, a young military officer who served many years in Canada, has given us some idea of the profits realized by French officials who engaged illegally in trade as silent partners. He has this to say of a local official at Montreal:

> *M. Perot, the governor of the town, who has but a thousand crowns a year salary, has made shift to get fifty thousand in a few years by trading with the savages in skins and furs.*

On a visit to the town of Three Rivers, he writes:

> *The king has made it the residence of a governor, who would die of hunger if he did not trade with the natives for beavers when his small allowance is out. Besides, a man who would live there must be of the like temper with a dog, or at least he must take pleasure in scratching his skin, for the fleas are there more numerous than the grains of sand.*

A serious evil began to grow out of the beaver trade—the tendency of Canada's most ambitious and vigorous young men to take to the woods as fur traders. Many of these bushrangers, or *coureurs de bois*, attracted by a life free of control by officials and priests, became more Indian than the Indians themselves. They abhorred the drudgery of tilling the soil and would have none of it. The forest was their home and the savages were their companions. They defeated the king's measures for increasing the population, for they did not marry French girls and raise families, but instead often formed a semimarital attachment in every tribe.

Some of these alliances proved lasting, resulting in many half-breeds, most of whom became completely Indian in character and manners. Their descendants remained a picturesque feature of the beaver trade long after England became sovereign in Canada.

On the whole, the *coureurs de bois* were a happy-go-lucky, reckless, lawless body of men. They roamed the wilderness all their days, following the beaver into unknown waters, the paddles of their canoes dripping to the rhythm of gay songs. Occasionally they emerged from the forest at some trading post, bedecked in face paint and a fantastic mixture of Indian and French finery, to barter their pelts and engage in a wild orgy till the last beaver skin had disappeared over the counter. At such times, they gave the authorities more trouble than the Indians did. Lahontan writes:

> *You would be amazed if you saw how lewd these pedlars are when they return; how they feast and game, and how prodigal they are, not only in their clothes, but upon women. They act just as our East Indiamen and pirates are wont to do, for they lavish, eat, drink, and play all away as long as the goods hold out; and when these are gone, they even sell their embroidery, their lace, and their clothes. This done, they are forced to go upon a new voyage for subsistence.*

The means of subsistence, a new stock of trade goods, usually had to be acquired on credit. It was a gay life.

Colonial governors tried repeatedly to regulate the activities of the *coureurs de bois*, but with little success. As their numbers grew, they were required to buy trading licenses, a requirement they usually flouted, although their gains were certainly great enough to bear such a tax. Lahontan makes this estimate of possible profit

The "coureurs de bois" roamed the wilderness all their days, following the beaver into unknown waters, the paddles of their canoes dipping to the rhythm of gay songs.

on the cargo of two canoes : "When the voyage is performed, this sum of a thousand crowns (the cost of the cargo) commonly brings in seven hundred percent clear profit, and sometimes more, sometimes less; for these sparks called *coureurs de bois* bite the savages most dexterously."

But the bushranger did not often grow rich; in fact he usually had little desire to grow rich. He was frequently only the agent of a trader who was permanently established at some post, and who supplied him on credit with the stock of goods he required for doing business. The trader took the cream and left very little milk for the bushranger. The few more ambitious men among them sometimes carried their pelts to Albany, where the Dutch gave them better prices than they could get from their own people.

For the Frenchman, trading at Albany was illegal, to be sure, but who was to stop him? A fig for the law! At one period, the intendant (the king's business manager) estimated that eight hundred men, nearly half the male population of Canada at that time, were scorning royal orders and living virtually as outlaws. The most severe penalties had no effect, for these men, buried in the wilds, were completely beyond control of the government. Some of them were further protected by being in secret partnership with high officials, who shared their illegal gains.

The famous Daniel Greysolon, Sieur Duluth, a man of good family and great ability, was for long the unofficial captain of the *coureurs de bois*. When two Indians once murdered a pair of French trappers near his post, he arrested them and assembled a private court that formally tried them. Found guilty, they were executed in the presence of four hundred angry fellow tribesmen, whom Duluth cowed when they threatened to free the prisoners. Indians respected Duluth, for he was always just and fair with them. He was trusted by French officials and performed important services for the colony. His name, which he himself spelled "Dulhut," is borne by the city of Duluth, Minnesota.

Another leader among the bushrangers was Nicolas Perrot, who single-handedly put down a raid of the Fox Indians against the Chippewas, firm friends of the French. Hearing that the Foxes were painting themselves for war and threatening to eat any Frenchman who interfered, Perrot walked boldly into their village, pointed his sword at his bared breast, and made an oration. "I hear," said he, "that you yearn to eat French flesh. Well, put the kettles on the fire. My flesh is white and savory, but it is very salty. If you eat it, it will not pass your Adam's apples before it vomits you!" The craving of the Foxes for human flesh passed at once. "You are our father," said the chief, "for you are the first who brought us iron. What child would eat its own father?"

At another time, a war party of Sioux, on a raid against the Foxes, chanced upon Perrot's camp and were about to plunder it. He secretly filled a cup with brandy, then pretended to fill it with water at a nearby stream. As he started to drink, he dropped a hot ember into the cup, which immediately burst into flames. "If you touch me or any of my men," he cried, "I will burn up all the lakes where you catch fish and the swamps where you gather wild rice." The Sioux left without harming him.

The Great River

Coureurs de bois who traded in the distant Great Lakes country brought back stories, told them by Indians, of a mighty river that flowed southward to the sea. The natives called it the "Father of Waters," the river that dwarfed all others. The Sioux, who lived on its upper reaches, called it the Messipi.

Count Frontenac, a new governor appointed in 1672 by Louis XIV, determined to send out an expedition to find and explore this father of waters. Its source, according to the Sioux, lay to the west of Lake Superior. If it existed at all, it must flow either to the Gulf of Mexico or to the "Sea of Virginia," the Atlantic. In either case, a fort at its mouth would prevent Spanish penetration from Mexico into the interior of the continent, and would open the river's entire course to the French fur trade.

Frontenac's choice as leader of his expedition was Louis Jolliet, an enterprising fur trader of Quebec, who was familiar with the shores of Lake Superior. Father Jacques Marquette, a Jesuit priest fluent in several Indian languages, was chosen to accompany him. Both were keen for the adventure. Jolliet, the man of business, hoped to open a vast new field for the fur trade. The priest's motives were quite different. At the beginning of his journal of the voyage he writes, "I found myself in the happy necessity of exposing my life for the salvation of all these tribes." These two intrepid men, so different in training and motive, proved to be a superb team.

With two light canoes and five *coureurs de bois*, they set out from Michilimackinac and cruised the northern shore of Lake Michigan to the southern end of Green Bay. Leaving the long-established mission at Green Bay on the seventeenth of May, 1673, they went by way of the Fox River to Lake Winnebago. From there friendly Indians guided them to the Wisconsin, which they followed to its mouth in the great river that was the object of their search. The Wisconsin town of Prairie du Chien now stands at this spot.

Turning south on the Mississippi, the party glided past wooded hills to vast prairies, where great herds of buffalo interrupted their grazing to stare at them. At length they reached the chief town of the Illinois Indians. They were welcomed with a flowery oration by the principal chief, who declared that their coming "added flavor to his tobacco, made the river more calm, the sky serene, and the earth more beautiful." Future visits of Frenchmen to the Illinois proved not to produce such beneficial results.

After many days of following the serpentine windings of the ever-growing Mississippi, they reached an Indian village at the mouth of the Arkansas. Here they suffered their last infliction of oratory and feasting. Marquette and Jolliet were now some seven hundred miles from the Mississippi's mouth, but believed they were much nearer. Their Indian hosts gave them fearsome reports of the bad hearts of the people in the lower reaches of the river. They had explored a great part of the stream they had set out to find, and had determined that it flowed to the Gulf of Mexico. Luck had been tempted far enough. They turned back and re-traced their route over the long miles to Green Bay, which they had quit four months earlier, having meanwhile paddled their canoes more than twenty-five hundred miles.

On some lonely reach of the lower Mississippi, they may have passed unknowingly over the spot where the body of Hernando de Soto had been consigned to a watery grave by his Spanish followers more than a century before. But the fact that de Soto was the first European to see the mighty Mississippi and that French trappers had cruised its northern headwaters in no way detracts from the honor due Louis Jolliet and Jacques Marquette.

The Sieur de La Salle

In the spring of 1666, a young man came out to New France whose name will always be linked with its fortunes, and whose exploits deeply affected its history. He was interested in the beaver trade principally as a means of financing his ambitious schemes for extending the borders of the colony. His ventures as a fur trader were not a success, largely because of the ill luck that dogged his footsteps, but partly through his habit of leaving the conduct of business affairs to subordinates while he roamed the forests. He died bankrupt and heavily in debt. His single ambition seems to have been the enlargement of the king's domains by exploration. To pursue this ambition, he gave up a life of prosperous ease in France to lead one of hardship and danger in the wilds of North America.

Robert Cavelier, Sieur de La Salle, was born of a wealthy and distinguished family at Rouen in Normandy. Granted a large tract of land fronting on the rapids above Montreal, he came out to Canada at the age of twenty-three, obsessed with the old dream of finding a shorter route to China. His enthusiasm for this idea led the wags of the town to give his seigneury the nickname of La Chine (China), a name now borne by the town that stands on its site, as well as by the rapids alongside.

La Salle's first ambition soon gave way to a new one. Marquette and Jolliet had made known a great part of the Mississippi, but they had not followed its course to the end, nor had they left any permanent bases for holding the country. La Salle would descend the river and assure control of its watershed by building forts at strategic points along the banks. Then he would build at its mouth a port from which the furs from this vast river system could be shipped to European markets. He would leave the beavers of the frozen north to the bushrangers, and lead French settlement and trade to the lush prairies bordering the Mississippi. Here was a project worthy of his most ambitious dreams! His heroic efforts to make that dream come true led to his own undoing, but they also led to French possession of the Mississippi Valley and a consequent tremendous extension of the fur traffic.

La Salle sold the seigneury of La Chine to finance his project, but kept another, called Fort Frontenac, recently granted him by the king, at the eastern end of Lake Ontario. His first move to secure the Mississippi's watershed was the building of Fort Crève-cœur on the Illinois River, near the present site of the city of Peoria. Nearby was the principal town of the Illinois Indians, a populous tribe who would become his first customers.

At the fort he planned to build a cargo boat for the voyage down the Mississippi. Crèvecœur, which means "broken heart," proved to be an apt name for the post. Soon after its completion and during La Salle's absence, the garrison mutinied, destroyed the fort, and deserted with all the trade goods they could carry. As if this were not enough hard luck, the Illinois town was sacked by the Iroquois, and all its people massacred or driven away.

A year passed before La Salle could recruit his forces and start his voyage down the Mississippi. He abandoned the plan of building a cargo boat, so his party dragged their canoes a hundred and fifty miles down the frozen Illinois River, where they managed to launch them among the floating ice floes of the Mississippi. After a voyage of more than three months down the great river, they split up to explore the three broad channels into which the river divided itself near the end of their journey. As La Salle's canoe swept around a last bend, the blue waters of the Gulf of Mexico spread to the horizon before his eyes.

On the ninth of April, 1682, La Salle, blithely disregarding any claims the present tenants might have, took formal possession for Louis XIV of all lands touched by the Mississippi and its tributary rivers. This was a domain reaching from the Appalachians to the Rockies, and from the headwaters of the Mississippi, Missouri, and Ohio to the Gulf of Mexico—a very large share of the continent of North America. He christened this immense area Louisiana, in honor of the king. A tree trunk bearing the arms of France was stuck in the ground, the party sang a sacred hymn, the soldiers fired a volley, and all shouted, "Vive le Roi!" A few local Indians, completely unaware of the significance of the ceremony, looked on in awestruck silence.

La Salle retraced his course up the Mississippi and Illinois and built another fort to replace the ruined Fort Crèvecœur. The new post, named Fort St. Louis, stood at the top of a cliff high above the Illinois River. The tribes settled near it in great numbers, welcoming a market for their beaver and a shield against the raids of the Iroquois. Tons of fur began to be brought into the post, and the ill luck that had dogged its proprietor's footsteps seemed to be turning into full-blown prosperity.

But fresh troubles appeared. Count Frontenac, the governor and La Salle's staunch supporter, was recalled to France. La Barre, the new governor, influenced by Montreal merchants afraid of losing the trade of the western tribes, turned against him. La Barre cut off all supplies, refused to send reinforcements for the weak garrison, and seized the seigneury of Fort Frontenac with all the furs stored there. Without sufficient trade goods and with only a few soldiers, La Salle would be unable either to hold the allegiance of his fickle neighbors or to assure them protection from their enemies.

In this unbearable situation, he determined to go to Paris and plead his case before the king. On his journey to Quebec he met an officer, sent by the governor, on his way to seize Fort St. Louis. This would seem to be the crowning disaster, but he pushed on to Quebec and sailed for France on the first available ship.

Fresh from years in the Canadian wilderness, La Salle stood before Louis XIV, the Sun King, and presented his case. It was received with favor beyond his hopes. He was commissioned governor of Louisiana, and an order was sent to La Barre commanding him to restore all of La Salle's seized property. Two small naval vessels and two cargo boats were assembled at Rochelle to carry the people and equipment necessary to found a colony at the mouth of the Mississippi. There were two hundred soldiers, as well as many mechanics and laborers. Two of La Salle's brothers, one of them a priest, and his nephew Moranget were among the volunteers, including thirty adventurous young men and several families with children. In addition, a number of unmarried girls joined the company, not unmindful, perhaps, of favorable matrimonial opportunities.

In high hopes, the fleet sailed near the end of July, 1684. Misfortune struck its first blow at the island of Santo Domingo, where one of the ships was captured by buccaneers. The three remaining vessels sighted land a few days after Christmas, a low marshy point on the shore of the Gulf of Mexico somewhere east of the Mississippi Delta.

Now began one of the most maddening of the long series of misadventures that beset the colony. When La Salle had descended the Mississippi by canoe nearly three years before, he had fixed the latitude of its mouth but had lacked instruments for determining longitude. So now the fleet was forced to sail west on a fixed line, somewhere along which lay their destination—exactly where, they did not know. They must locate the mouth of the river by sight, a very difficult thing to do along a flat coast indented by many bays and inlets.

After many days of westward cruising, they sighted an inlet which La Salle identified as the place they were looking for. The colonists went ashore in small boats and the two supply ships were ordered to go through the inlet and anchor in the bay at its head. Coming through the narrow channel, one of them went aground on a reef. Battered unmercifully by the surf, she soon went to pieces, leaving the surrounding water strewn with the boxes and bales of her cargo. As the waves cast the precious stores on the beach, a band of Indians rushed out of the bushes and began to carry them away. After driving off the looters, the disconsolate company made a camp of sorts amid what stores they were able to salvage, and Captain Beaujeu, the naval commander, sailed away in his one remaining ship. He had offered to go to Martinique, a French possession, to summon help, but La Salle, who had quarreled with him from the start, declined his offer. The other cargo boat, the *Belle*, remained with the colony.

After a few days' exploration of the neighboring wilderness, La Salle realized that he had been mistaken; this was not the mouth of his river. It was not the mouth of any river at all. It was in fact the entrance to what is now Matagorda Bay, nearly five hundred miles beyond the Mississippi's delta. These city-bred people, sick and discouraged by their misfortunes, were in no condition to go on at once. They must be provided for here, while La Salle himself found a site for permanent settlement. On a bit of high ground at the head of the bay, they built a rough camp called Fort St. Louis, which was to be their temporary home. For most of them, it proved to be their final resting place.

Two long and disastrous attempts by La Salle to locate the Mississippi resulted only in the death of many of his men and the loss of the *Belle* with nearly all her crew. As a last resort, the company might have crowded into her and made their way to Martinique. The four hundred people who had sailed so hopefully from Rochelle had dwindled to forty-five. The only hope of rescue now lay in getting word of their plight to Quebec, and their leader started on a last, desperate attempt to go there.

Week after week his small rescue party, rain-drenched and hungry, struggled through swampy forests, determined to find the fatal river which, they had by now learned from Indians, lay far to the east. When they had found it, they would make canoes and paddle a thousand miles up the Mississippi, Illinois, and on through the Great Lakes to Quebec, where word of the desperate situation of the colony could be sent to Paris. Surely the king would send a ship posthaste to rescue their friends at Matagorda.

Some of the men La Salle had chosen to go with him on this rescue mission had been driven to the point of mutiny by their past misfortunes, for which they blamed the leader. One afternoon, they made camp beside a little river and sent out a hunting party, which succeeded in shooting two buffalo. After hanging the meat over a fire to dry, the hunters sent for horses to carry it to camp, which was several miles away. When the horses arrived in care of Moranget, La Salle's nephew, a violent quarrel flared up. The hot-tempered Moranget berated two of the hunters for having eaten some of the choice meat. This tirade fanned their smoldering hate of him and they secretly determined to take revenge.

That night, as they lay waiting for the meat to dry, the plotters murdered the sleeping Moranget and two other loyal men. The assassins then realized that their only hope of safety lay in adding the death of La Salle to their crimes.

The main party, camped on the river, grew anxious when the hunters had not returned a day after they were due, and La Salle went in search of them. As he approached their bivouac, two of the mutineers, hidden in the tall grass, fired at the same moment, and the valiant survivor of so many perils fell dead in the marsh. They stripped the corpse of its tattered garments and left it there for the vultures.

After some weeks of aimless wandering, with the honest members of the party in fear of their lives, the two ringleaders of the mutineers got into a violent fight and were killed by some of their companions or perhaps murdered each other. The remaining renegades decided to cast their lot permanently with the savages, but allowed the loyal men to leave them and go where they pleased. These remnants of La Salle's shining adventure at length reached Quebec and sailed for France. The king sent an order for the arrest of the murderers, long buried in the wilderness, but left the colonists at Matagorda to their fate.

Some three years after this, a Spanish force from Mexico found the scene of the colony's final agony. The camp lay in ruins, and the only sign of the inhabitants was three corpses lying on the prairie. The Spanish commander learned that a few refugees were held by a nearby tribe, and rescued them. They told a gruesome story. Three months before, Indians had attacked the camp and butchered all except themselves. The Spaniards took those they

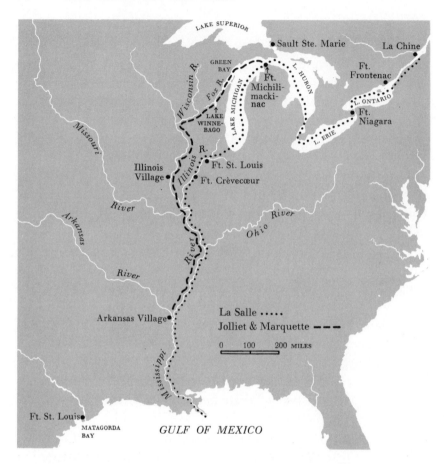

The Great Lakes and the Mississippi Valley region, showing Jolliet and Marquette's exploration of the Mississippi, 1673, and La Salle's exploration of the Mississippi, 1679.

had rescued to Mexico, where two of them later joined the Spanish navy. Serving aboard a man-of-war that was captured by the French, they at long last reached home. With the exception of the small group of loyal men who completed the terrible journey back to Quebec, they were the only members of the ill-fated Matagorda colony who ever again saw their native land.

Down the Mississippi
and Toward the Western Sea

Ten years after La Salle's tragic failure, a far luckier expedition gained a permanent foothold at the mouth of the Mississippi. The Sieur d'Iberville, a native of Montreal serving as an admiral in the French navy, was sent from France with four ships loaded with people and equipment to plant a colony in lower Louisiana. The first settlement was made at the present site of Biloxi, Mississippi. Iberville, cruising along the coast westward from Biloxi, found the Mississippi's delta and explored it.

When he was later ordered to naval duty elsewhere, his younger brother Bienville succeeded to the command of the colony and in 1718 founded New Orleans. This settlement grew rapidly and soon became the outlet for the furs shipped from recently established French posts much farther up the river. Principal centers of the upriver trade were Cahokia, near the present site of St. Louis, and an island in the Mississippi at the mouth of the Kaskaskia River. The pelts from these posts, loaded on large bateaux, were floated down to New Orleans and from there shipped to France.

In 1763 Pierre Laclede, partner in a New Orleans trading firm, toiled for three months up the river with a bateau-load of trade goods to establish a post in the Illinois country. With him was his fourteen-year-old stepson, René Auguste Chouteau.

For the location of his post, which he named St. Louis, Laclede chose a site on the west bank of the Mississippi a few miles below the mouth of the Missouri. Young René, after his father's death, became head of the business, and with his half brother Jean Pierre developed it into the most successful of the early St. Louis fur companies, a position it held for many years. The prosperity of this company was largely responsible for the early growth of St. Louis, which later became the great center of the United States' fur trade. This was the jumping-off place of the American beaver trappers, the "mountain men," for their advance across the prairies to the Rocky Mountains and the Pacific Coast.

Meanwhile the fur dealers of eastern Canada, financial strength of the colony, began to feel the bite of western competition. The trapper necessarily uses up his raw material in the course of business, and usually pays little attention to the conservation of his stock. Early trappers—and later ones as well—took all the pelts they could collect from any district and then moved on. There would always be plenty of beavers farther west, they reasoned. By the time the Mississippi Valley was beginning to be exploited, beavers had become too scarce along the St. Lawrence to make large-scale trapping profitable.

To the north was the powerful English Hudson's Bay Company, which had for many years been operating from Hudson Bay, barring that area to the French. To the south were the hostile Iroquois, who traded at Albany their own catch and that of their neighbors farther west, for whom they acted as middlemen. The English settlements in New England made trapping in that quarter impossible. Even the Great Lakes region, where there had been a seemingly inexhaustible supply of raw material, now furnished comparatively few pelts. The Algonquin and Huron nations, chief suppliers of beaver to the St. Lawrence posts, had been scattered to the four winds by the Iroquois. Decimated and dispirited by this disaster and by the ravages of smallpox, they no longer came down the Ottawa with great fleets of canoes loaded to the gunwale with pelts. Beaver furs from the posts along the Mississippi were being shipped down the river to New Orleans. If Canada was to survive, her trappers must follow the beaver to new hunting grounds to the west and northwest of the Great Lakes.

The first French beaver hunters known to have ventured into the country around the headwaters of the Mississippi were Pierre Esprit Radisson, probably the first European since de Soto to see the great river, and Médard Chouart, Sieur de Groseilliers, his brother-in-law. From a winter's trapping west of Lake Superior they brought back to Montreal a fine haul of "black beaver," thick dark-colored pelts that brought a premium price. They suffered fines and confiscation of their furs, because of trapping without having first made undercover arrangements with grafting officials.

After the news of their successful hunt became known along the St. Lawrence, so many young men hustled out to the new grounds that Talon, the intendant, feared the colony would be depopulated. He ruled that any unmarried trapper going west must marry a French girl before his departure as a pledge for his return. This powerful lure was partially successful, for the *coureur de bois*, for all his carefree ways, could be a good husband and strongly attached to his family. Pierre Radisson, after describing the hardships and loneliness of life in the wilderness, writes feelingly of the joy of returning home,

> *when one sees his own chimney smoak, or when he can kisse his own wife or kisse his neighbor's wife with ease and delight. It is a different thing when victuals are wanting, worke whole nights and dayes, lye down on the bare ground, and not always that hap; the breech in the water, the feare in the buttocks, to have the belly empty, the weariness in the bones, the drowsiness in the body by the bad weather you are to suffer, having nothing to keep you from such calamity.*

Many of those who acquired wives under this ruling of Talon's did return to them, bringing not only numerous packs of pelts, but wonderful tales of blond Indians who grew beards, rode horses, and wore armor, who had never seen a canoe, had no wood, and cooked over fires of dry buffalo dung. There were mountains of stone, so the stories ran, that glistened day and night, the "Shining Mountains." These western trappers had been told of a great river that Indians had followed west to a large lake whose water was salty, and whose surface regularly rose and fell. This at last must be the siren that had lured so many dreamers, the Northwest Passage! And, best of all, the streams were so crowded with beaver that the natives placed very little value on pelts, but threw away robes used for clothing before they were worn out and replaced them with new ones.

Such tales at length influenced the authorities at Quebec to send out an expedition to report on this fabulous country, to explore new trapping grounds, and to make another search for that elusive water route to the Pacific.

The king's minister in Paris was not enthusiastic about the proposal. Too much money had already been drained from the royal treasury in the search for a water route to the Pacific. The minister suggested that His Majesty was more interested in finding a sea of beaver than in finding any other sea.

But the originator of the project and its chief promoter, the Sieur de La Vérendrye, agreed to conduct the expedition without expense to the king, provided he be granted a monopoly of the western trade as a means of financing the adventure. The king deigned to grant this, but refused to advance any cash.

La Vérendrye belonged to a prominent but impoverished family of the town of Three Rivers, on the St. Lawrence below Montreal. He had fought well for France in Europe and carried the scars of nine wounds. The king appointed him commander of trading posts on Lake Nipigon, north of Lake Superior, and on the strength of his monopoly he formed a partnership of local merchants.

With pomp and ceremony, La Vérendrye marched out of Montreal in the summer of 1731. With him were three of his sons, his nephew La Jemmeraye, fifty *voyageurs*, and a few artisans and carpenters. They made their way steadily westward, trapping beaver and building fortified posts on Rainy Lake and Lake Winnipeg. Here they spent the second winter out from Montreal, narrowly avoiding starvation on a diet of roots, rawhide, and hunting dogs. Game had deserted their vicinity, and they could catch no fish through the ice.

Part of the third winter was spent with the Mandan Indians at their towns on the Missouri River near where Bismarck, North Dakota, now stands. After a long stay with these friendly people, La Vérendrye, worn and disheartened, returned to Fort La Reine, a post he had built on the Assiniboine River just south of Lake Manitoba. He had found no river flowing to the west, and the furs he had gathered and sent back to Montreal all went toward settling his debts. His nephew Jemmeraye had died, and his eldest son, Jean

Baptiste, camped on an island in Lake of the Woods, had been surprised by the Sioux Indians and massacred with twenty of his men. As a taunting gesture, the savages had left the bodies of their victims carefully wrapped in beaver skins.

From Fort La Reine, two of La Vérendrye's younger sons, François and Louis Joseph, set out on another westward exploration, inspired by Indian stories of white men who lived in houses of stone and whose country was only a short march from the sea. It is more than likely that the Indians who inhabited the countryside through which they were passing, out of fear of these strange men, told them provocative tall tales merely to hasten them on their way.

Going again to the Mandan towns on the Missouri, the brothers procured guides and struck out afoot to the southwest, eventually joining an Indian war party which traveled with full equipment: tepees, horse herds, squaws, papooses, and dogs. This motley rabble was on its way to attack an enemy tribe known to them as the Snake People. In company with these unsavory companions, the two young La Vérendryes continued westward, and after many days' travel approached a towering range of mountains. From its top, they were told, the western ocean could be seen. The mountains were probably the Black Hills of South Dakota, and the Pacific was more than a thousand miles farther west.

As they neared the range the women made camp, for the enemy town was near. The doughty warriors went on to the attack, but when they reached the village they found it deserted. The Snake People, terrified at the approach of the hostile band, had fled into the hills. Panic also seized the attackers. Fearful that the enemy had flanked them and was at that moment ravaging their camp, they hastened back to the defense of their squaws and horses. The retreat soon became a rout, which kept on going after the unharmed squaws had been picked up. So the brothers were cheated, or so they fancied, of a sight of the sea they had come so far to find.

By now the La Vérendryes had had their fill of exploring and started back on the long march to Fort La Reine. An account of the journey, written after their return, is so indefinite as to locations and distances that it is impossible to fix their exact route, but they undoubtedly had penetrated farther into the unknown west than any white man before them. When they reached the Missouri on their return march, they buried a lead plate, given to their father by the viceroy, which had been carried on all their travels. On it was engraved in Latin, "In the 26th year of the reign of Louis XV the most illustrious Lord, the Lord Marquis de Beauharnois being viceroy, 1741, Pierre de La Vérendrye placed this." To this inscription his sons added, "Placed by the La Vérendryes March 30, 1743." Seventy years later, near Pierre, South Dakota, this plate was accidentally dug up by schoolchildren at play.

After all these heroic efforts for the colony, the elder La Vérendrye was dismissed from his command of the forts he had built in the Northwest. His authority was later restored, but he died soon afterward. It was left for others to harvest the furs of the new beaver country to which he had shown the way.

Events were now in the making that halted forever the march of France across North America. Age-old enmities in Europe brought on the Seven Years' War, which had its counterpart in America in the French and Indian War. Lord Jeffrey Amherst, the British commander, took the forts of Louisburg and Ticonderoga, and the weaker posts in the West fell to his subordinates. The contest narrowed to a struggle for the St. Lawrence strongholds. The climax came when a British army under General James Wolfe rowed silently down the river by night and scaled the cliffs that Jacques Cartier and his handful of Breton sailors had climbed long ago.

Montcalm, the French commander, awakened the next morning to find Wolfe's army drawn up in line of battle outside the fortress that he had believed to be impregnable. The French were compelled to come out and meet the attack on the Plains of Abraham, where they were completely defeated. Both commanders lost their lives in the battle. Montreal fell soon after, and the war was over. The Treaty of Paris that followed in 1763 ended French dominion in Canada, as well as in Louisiana, which was ceded to Spain.

From the time when Breton fishermen traded fishhooks and brass buttons for beaver skins at Anticosti Island, till the march of the La Vérendryes to the Black Hills of South Dakota, two hundred years had passed. During that span, the adventurous and carefree bush-rangers of New France had blazed a trail two thirds of the way across a continent. The lure that sparked their march, and the wealth that made it possible, had come from the lowly rodent whose fur was good material for making hats. The trail to the West had been paved with the bleaching bones of the beaver.

III

GENTLEMEN ADVENTURERS

The Great Company

IN 1610 HENRY HUDSON, VETERAN OF THREE VOY-
ages to North America, sailed under the flag of England in search
of the Northwest Passage. On this his fourth attempt to find the
fabled waterway, he entered the great inland sea that we know
as Hudson Bay. After spending fruitless months searching for an
outlet from it leading to the west, his ship was frozen in for the
winter. When spring came, his starving crew mutinied and set him
adrift, with his son and eight loyal men, in a small boat without
food or water. They were never heard of again. The mutinous
crew turned the ship about and eventually reached home. On the
strength of this tragic voyage, England based her claim to all
territory touching Hudson Bay, but she did nothing about occupying the bleak country for many years.

We have seen how the Frenchmen Radisson and Groseilliers,
trapping to the southwest of Hudson Bay, suffered the loss of their
fine catch to grafting officials. The two ambitious trappers were
much disgruntled, as well they might have been, by the action of
the Canadian authorities. They had found a wealth of beaver,
however, and sought more sympathetic backers for another attempt in the same general area. Going to London, they persuaded
a number of nobles at the court of Charles II to form a trading
company to operate out of Hudson Bay.

The chance that a waterway might be found leading out of this
arm of the Atlantic to the western sea was an added inducement
dangled before the eyes of the aristocratic shareholders, who

64

might have considered it beneath their dignity to engage in commerce.

In 1670 the playboy king, influenced by his cronies at court under the leadership of his cousin, Prince Rupert, granted a very favorable charter to the "Governor and Company of Adventurers of England Trading into Hudson's Bay." It gave the company complete monopoly of the fur trade, as well as practically sovereign rights over all territory touched by the rivers draining into the great bay.

In return for this, the company bound itself to look for a water route to the Pacific, and to give the sovereign of England, whenever he might happen to enter their territory, two elks and two black beavers. Charles II never made himself eligible to collect this bounty, nor did many other English sovereigns. But Elizabeth II, on her first visit to Canada as queen, was presented a handsome beaver coat in place of the live animals.

The gentlemen adventurers did not themselves venture into this savage expanse of lakes, rivers, and muskeg over which their charter made them masters, but Radisson and Groseilliers, as managers for the company, ventured into it promptly. The first post they built, Fort Charles, was located on the shore of James Bay, the southern arm of Hudson Bay. Other posts were later built at the mouths of the Moose, Albany, Severn, and Nelson Rivers. During its early years, the policy followed by the company was to maintain fixed trading "factories" on the coast, with the Indians doing the trapping in the wilderness and bringing their pelts down the rivers to them.

The French authorities in Canada did not view this activity with unqualified approval. At this time, British control of Canada was more than ninety years in the future, and Canada considered Hudson Bay and its surrounding country to be part of her domain. As a result, there was much capturing and recapturing of these forts, whether England and France happened to be at war or at peace.

After a few years, Radisson and Groseilliers, dissatisfied with the waiting-at-the-coast policy of the company they had helped

*Tempting goods were offered for sale at the trading posts, such
as blankets, knives, guns, beads, ribbons, tea and kettles.*

organize, and denied a share in its profits, went back to French service. Radisson in 1682 led a raid that seized the company's post at the mouth of the Nelson River, and a few years later a foray from Montreal took the three posts on James Bay. Both proved to be temporary conquests; in time the bases were regained by the company through diplomacy. This unofficial warfare went on until 1713, when the treaty that ended the War of the Spanish Succession in Europe gave all the country around Hudson Bay to England.

Even though the Hudson's Bay men did not go into the forests to trade, the posts on the coast did a thriving business from the start. Nearby Indians and many from much farther west, attracted by the quality and prices of the English merchandise, came down the rivers every summer, their canoes loaded with the prime pelts grown by the beavers in this cold northern land.

The English had little stomach for the hardships and perils of the winter wilderness. Who can blame them for preferring to sit by their blazing fires, so long as customers came to them in satisfactory numbers? This was forbidding country at best, and in winter it was enough to try the soul of any man. Hoarfrost covered the interior walls of rooms where roaring fires were burning; the soil was frozen five feet down, and only a few inches of the top thawed in the short summers.

An Indian arriving at one of these posts carried his fur into the receiving room, where an experienced clerk, after counting and grading the pelts, gave him tally sticks notched to indicate the number and quality of the skins he had turned in. Then the customer took his sticks to the trading room, where he could wander along the long rows of tempting goods offered for sale: blankets, knives, cloth, axes, guns, lead, powder, and flints; luxuries such as beads, ribbons, tea, paint, kettles, and all the other fascinating articles that the simple people of the forest had learned to crave. A family man or a young buck often brought a shopping list of things he hoped would appeal to his squaw.

Then there was rum, which always commanded a good share of the pelts. The final sentence of an old report reads, "Brandy goes off incomparably well." The entire way of life of these Stone-Age people was being altered by the manufactured goods that they could buy with a few beaver pelts.

When the customer had made his selection, he paid in notched sticks, each notch worth one "made pelt," meaning a cured skin in good condition stretched on a tree limb bent in the shape of a horseshoe. Prices, of course, varied from time to time and at different posts. The typical trading value of one prime pelt might be a half pound of colored beads; one brass kettle; a half pound of powder; two pounds of shot; one hatchet; eight jackknives; one pound of Brazil tobacco. A coat made of blanket material might cost twelve pelts; a gun, ten or more, depending on its quality.

The trader was usually wary of selling firearms and ammunition to Indians. There was no objection if he could be sure the weapon would be used against rival traders, or against tribes that patronized a competitor. But there was always the possibility that a gun sold at any post might someday send a bullet back home where it came from.

These prices represented a tremendous margin of profit. During its first twenty years, the company paid to its shareholders 295 percent on the original price of their shares. The gentlemen adventurers were doing very well.

But business with local tribes began to fall off as overtrapping diminished the supply of beavers. The former stream of western customers diminished. There were many reasons. Recurrent wars in Europe, each with its accompanying small war in America, choked off the supply of trade goods. The richest trapping country now lay to the west of Lake Superior, where new French posts on Lake Nipigon and Rainy Lake lured western Indians on their way to trade with the English. These French posts now got the lion's share of the pelts that had formerly gone to the bay. Also, there was much adverse criticism in Parliament, where the company was censured for neglect of its charter obligation to explore the country.

After the three posts on James Bay were captured by the French, the company built posts farther north, and began of necessity to take more interest in going into the field. This was done partly to convince Parliament that they were trying to find the Northwest Passage, but its principal object was to initiate trade.

In 1690 the governor of York Factory, located where the Nelson and Hayes Rivers flow into Hudson Bay, sent out a traveling salesman named Henry Kelsey, a nineteen-year-old servant of the company. In contrast to the general run of Hudson's Bay employees, who despised the "dirty savages," Kelsey liked Indians, loved their roving way of life, and was fascinated by their wild country. He fancied himself a poet, but wrote rather bad doggerel.

Kelsey set out from York Factory with a party of Cree Indians, who were returning to their homes on the shore of Lake Winnipeg, three hundred miles away. Arriving at length at this huge lake, he went on up the Saskatchewan River, the first European to see the stream that was to become the great trappers' highway to the far Northwest. Still lured by the fascination of the wilderness, he went beyond Lake Manitoba to the country of the Assiniboins, with whom he spent the winter.

During the following summer, he wandered over the great plains of Saskatchewan, and may even have seen from a distance the Rocky Mountains. He must at least have heard about them from his Indian friends. Everywhere he went he set forth in glowing terms the attractions of the long journey to the trading posts on Hudson Bay, but the Plains tribes did not respond with any great enthusiasm.

After another winter on the prairies he returned to York Factory, having been absent more than two years. Although he had been the first to explore what came to be one of the most important territories in fur-trade history, he got no reward from his employers, and they made no use of the information he gathered.

Kelsey's written account of the journey says simply, "I had my labor for my travel." He was the first European to see the great western prairies, to marvel at the tremendous herds of buffalo, and to experience the life of the horse-riding Plains Indians. He wrote a poem about his encounter with an animal never before mentioned by a white man. Discarding poetry in his formal report, he describes the beast as "a great sort of Bear which is bigger than any white Bear and neither White nor Black but silver hair'd like our English Rabbit." Thus the grizzly bear makes its debut in literature.

The company persisted in neglecting the information that Kelsey had brought back. Meanwhile Pierre La Vérendrye and his French successors at Lake Nipigon had built a chain of fortified posts that cut squarely across the trade routes to Hudson Bay, and they got most of the pelts. The Indians saw no point in traveling several hundred miles farther than was necessary to do their shopping. Business at the bay continued to fall off, and share-holders began to complain about the meager dividends. But the company officers were not yet convinced that their policy of "let the customers come to us" no longer worked.

A young employee at York Factory named Anthony Henday was now given the thankless job of trying to wean the western Crees and Assiniboins away from their attachment to the French traders. He had no success whatever. Everywhere he went, he found the natives loyal to their old friends, who lived among them, shared their hard lives, and claimed kinship by maintaining wives in various tribes. Like Kelsey, Henday liked the life he was leading and kept going west for sheer love of adventure. His wanderings led him up the South Saskatchewan and its fork, the Red Deer, all the way to the Rocky Mountains of southern Alberta. With the possible exception of Kelsey, he is the first Englishman known to have seen the great range.

Henday wintered with the Blackfeet, a tribe of southern Al-berta, who were later to become a thorn in the flesh of most fur trappers. These Indians showed even less enthusiasm for the thou-sand-mile journey to Hudson Bay than had the tribes farther east. When Henday got back to York Factory, his report finally convinced the company officers that they would have to break away from the coast and establish new posts where the customers were.

But events soon made it unnecessary for them to woo the Indians away from French competition. Lord Jeffrey Amherst won his war, and all Canada passed to the ownership of England. Other competition later appeared in plenty, but it did not come from a possession of France.

The Scots Move In

After Bonnie Prince Charlie's forlorn bid for the British throne had met its end on Culloden Moor, many of his Scottish followers had fled to Canada. Some of them settled in Montreal and eventually became powers in the fur trade. Their full-flavored Highland names—McGillivray, McDonald of Garth, Finlay, McTavish—came to be spoken with respect in many a forest trading post.

These Scots proved to be better woodsmen than their Hudson's Bay Company competitors, more resourceful in the wilderness and more adept in dealing with savage customers. They had no qualms about venturing into the Northwest country, which they began to invade in considerable numbers after the English conquest of Canada. Company men contemptuously called these independent traders "pedlars," but they prospered, and their energetic competition cut still further into the business of the posts on Hudson Bay.

Though the Scots were shrewd traders, they never mastered the skills necessary for navigating treacherous wilderness rivers in frail birchbark canoes. The French *voyageurs* were master rivermen, and the Scots of necessity depended on them to man their boats. Canoe fleets supplying northwestern traders followed the familiar route that led from Montreal up the Ottawa and through Lake Huron to the western end of Lake Superior. From there it led westward along what came to be called the Northwest Road, a chain of small lakes and rivers that led to the country around Lake Winnipeg. The present boundary between the United States and Canada follows this old canoe route from Lake Superior to Lake of the Woods.

The *voyageur* was usually a completely illiterate half-breed who signed his name with an *X*, but he was not lacking in intelligence and was blessed with a gay spirit. In his picturesque but grimy clothes, plying his paddle to the cadence of a song, he made a holiday of running a perilous sault or carrying a back-breaking load over a portage.

The *voyageur* was much given to song. It was an expression of his carefree spirit, an antidote for his loneliness, and a means of timing his paddle strokes. His tunes were mostly Old World folk melodies, often set to new lyrics by some forest ballad maker— and often completely unfit for publication. Not always, however. Many were innocent pastoral ballads loaded with rustic sentiment. One of the most popular, carried on the breeze over a thousand wilderness lakes, was "At the Clear Fountain."

The "voyageurs" were much given to song. One may imagine the astonishment of a bull moose at the sound of a dozen lusty voices.

"À la claire fontaine   "At the clear fountain
    M'en allant promener,   As I strolled idly by,
J'ai trouvé l'eau si belle   The cool sparkling water
    Que je m'y suis baigné.   Said, Come bathe in me.
Il y a longtemps que je t'aime,   Long have I loved you,
    Jamais je ne t'oublierai."   Ne'er forgot will you be."

One may imagine the astonishment of a bull moose, feeding at dusk in the shallows along shore, as he lifted his head from the water and pricked up his ears at the sound of a dozen lusty voices singing "The Lovely Lysette," "Black-eyed Marie Whose Skirts Fly Up," or "I'm Plenty Scared of Those Hungry Wolves."

It required iron muscles and great skill to maneuver a heavily loaded canoe over these wild rivers and windy lakes. Take, for example, the thousand-mile obstacle course from Montreal to Grand Portage, on the western shore of Lake Superior. A Montreal convoy could expect to reach Grand Portage in about forty-five days, a backbreaking run on which there were thirty-six portages. Starting from La Chine with a rousing farewell, the crews always stopped at the chapel of Ste. Anne de Bellevue, at the mouth of the Ottawa, to pray for the protection of their patron saint during the voyage. This is the chapel mentioned in Thomas Moore's lovely poem "Canadian Boat Song."

> *"Faintly as tolls the evening chime,*
>   *Our voices keep tune and our oars keep time,*
>   *Soon as the woods on the shore grow dim*
>   *We'll sing at Ste. Anne's our parting hymn,*
>   *Row, brothers, row! The stream runs fast,*
>   *The rapids are near and the daylight's past."*

For a full season's hard, dangerous work, a *voyageur* might be paid two hundred and fifty livres, the equivalent of perhaps eighty or ninety dollars today. If he was strong enough to carry more than the usual two packs over a portage, or good at leading a song, he might be paid a bit more than this princely wage. Of course, he got his board and lodging free: hominy and hot grease for board, and ground space under an overturned canoe for lodging. On special occasions, such as the finish of a particularly rough portage or the end of a long voyage, he might be given the additional reward of a swallow of brandy.

But in spite of danger, hard work, and small pay, the *voyageur's* devil-may-care spirit and pride of skill made for a high degree of morale. On a portage the men strove to outdo one another merely to prove their manhood. On favorable water, the canoes of a convoy often engaged in a race, each crew paddling swiftly to reach the next portage ahead of all the others.

In the rare event of one convoy's overtaking another, a wild race was sure to follow. One such contest lasted for forty-eight hours, with the crews paddling at top speed during all that time. Toward the finish, one exhausted paddler went to sleep and tumbled overboard. None of the other contestants would interrupt their progress long enough to pick him up, and his own crew mates finally had to turn back to haul their half-drowned comrade out of the water.

The great advantage of the birchbark canoe was its light weight. Two men could carry one of average size with ease, yet it would support a heavy load and responded miraculously to a twist of the steersman's paddle. Heavy boats could never have been carried over the many long, rough portages. The principal disadvantage of the birch canoe was its frailty. The slightest error in judgment while running a rapid might throw it against a boulder and rip a gash in its bottom. If it went under, those lucky enough to reach shore fished the unlucky ones out of quiet water below the rapids and buried them on the bank. Many a sault was marked with rude crosses, erected over the graves of its victims. If the damaged craft remained afloat until it could be beached, repair material was usually close at hand. A section of bark stripped from a nearby white birch could be sewed with watap, pliable spruce roots, over the damaged area, and the edges of the patch made waterproof with a coating of pine resin.

The canoe's frame was made of white cedar, a light, tough wood.

Sections of bark fitted over the frame were sewn in place and all joints treated with resin, a waterproofing that did not last long and had to be renewed frequently. Most *voyageurs* were skilled canoe makers and could readily repair a damaged craft. The high prow was usually decorated with a crude design painted in garish colors.

The many small lakes of the Northwest Road are blue gems set in forests of evergreen and hardwood, but the *voyageur* doubtless took small notice of their beauty. He was too busy. Roused from sleep beneath his overturned canoe before daybreak, he break-fasted on hominy or wild rice heated in melted fat, loaded his canoe, and was off for twelve or more hours of hard toil. If a following wind happened to be blowing over quiet water, a tar-paulin might be rigged as a sail. While the breeze lasted, the paddler could sit and smoke his pipe as the canoe raced along at perhaps seven miles an hour.

The usual paddling cadence on lakes was about forty strokes a minute, which propelled the craft at from five to six miles an hour in calm weather. At this rate, up to a hundred miles could be covered in a long day if no carries were necessary. A portage might require an hour or the better part of a day, depending on its length and character. Many were only a few hundred yards long. One of the longest, the Grand Portage, was nine miles from end to end.

When a canoe was beached at the beginning of a portage, it was immediately unloaded and the bow man and the steerer hoisted it on their shoulders and went ahead, followed by the crew, each carrying two ninety-pound packs. The average-sized canoe pro-vided room for twenty-eight or thirty packs. A huge Negro named Pierre Bonga, famous among his fellows, could carry four packs, nearly twice his own weight.

On easy portages, the men went at a dogtrot; over difficult ones they might have to crawl up steep banks or wade through miry swamps. At one roundly cursed carry, called the Staircase, the men had to climb a series of footholds cut into an almost vertical rock ledge. Broken bones, sprained ankles, and minor injuries were

commonplace at most portages. At certain rapids, the partly unloaded canoe had to be towed at the end of a rope by men walking
alongshore or wading near the bank. This was called "cordelling."
Other rapids could be passed without unloading, the canoe being
pushed along with iron-tipped setting poles.

When, after long weeks of toil, a convoy approached its destination, the *voyageurs* donned their Sunday clothes, which had been
stowed in waterproof bags throughout the voyage. With the crews
gaily arrayed in blue capotes, red caps decorated with feathers,
gaudy sashes, and scarlet leggings, the canoes swept triumphantly
into port in single file, amid a welcoming uproar of shouting men,
shrieking squaws, and barking dogs. Then everybody got drunk
and danced all night.

The Scottish "pedlars" from Montreal rapidly extended their
trading far to the north of Lake Winnipeg, to country where
winter lasted for eight or nine months and normal temperature was
thirty degrees below zero, with frequent spells of *cold* weather.
But beavers were as thick as fleas and wore handsome coats of dark,
luxurious fur. The long summer days were mild, with the sun
shining through much of the night. In this far north country
game was scarce, but the lakes teemed with fish of many varieties:
whitefish, lake trout, pike, carp, and sturgeon. Camp helpers
worked long hours at the seines during the short summer, and
packed the catch in icehouses. The men had almost nothing else to
eat all winter, a bill of fare that doubtless failed to tempt their
jaded appetites, but either they ate fish or they didn't eat at all.

The rivers and lakes were free of ice for only a few months, and
while they were open all pelts had to be carried to the nearest
depot and trade goods and supplies brought back. The distance
from some of the posts to Grand Portage, the supply depot for all
the Northwest country, was so great that it required an entire
summer season to make the round trip. The buildings of this post
were located on the shore of Lake Superior a few miles from the
present site of Fort William, Ontario. Here was the long carry that
led to the beginning of the Northwest Road.

In this lonely northern wilderness all hands, from the boss (known as the *bourgeois*) down to the humblest kitchen helper, sought the solace of female companionship. The women of some tribes, especially those of mixed French and Indian blood, were often attractive, dressed in their white doeskin shifts ornamented with colored porcupine quills, their faces tinted with vermilion, and their black hair arranged in great coils decorated with glass beads. Daniel Harmon, a young Vermonter of somewhat straitlaced background, after six years of wrestling with his conscience, made this entry in his journal :

> *This day a Canadian's daughter, a girl of about four-teen years of age, was offered to me, and after mature considera-tion concerning the step which I ought to take, I have finally concluded to accept her, as it is customary for all gentlemen who remain for any length of time in this part of the world to have a female companion with whom they can pass their time more sociably and agreeably than to live a lonely life, as they must do if single. If we can live in harmony together my intention now is to keep her as long as I remain in this uncivilized part of the world, and when I return to my native land I shall endeavor to place her under the protection of some honest man, with whom she can pass the remainder of her days much more agree-ably than it would be possible for her to do were she to be taken down into the civilized world, to manners, customs and lan-guages of which she would be an entire stranger. The girl is said to have a mild disposition and an even temper, which are quali-ties very necessary to make an agreeable woman and an affec-tionate partner.*

His scruples in this delicate matter were not shared by many of his hard bitten fellows, most of whom casually bought or sold their female companions. Harmon did not hold to his plan to leave his helpmate "under the protection of some honest man." He grew to be genuinely fond of her, and eventually took her and their two little daughters to his native Vermont village, where they lived out a long life together and reared a family of ten children. Many another of these temporary arrangements led to permanent attachments.

The Nor'westers

As the competition from Montreal increased, additional worries for the Hudson's Bay Company appeared. Traders from Albany began to invade the Northwest, as well as Frenchmen from Kaskaskia in the Illinois country. The repeated attempts by company agents to lure reluctant western Indians to Hudson Bay continued to be disappointing; the traders who went out into the woods got a great deal of the business.

One of these company drummers, Samuel Hearne, had been sent out twice to stir up trade, with the additional side job of doing some exploring. There were rumors of a big river somewhere in the Northwest that ran through country rich in pure copper. It might lead to the long-sought waterway to China. On his third attempt to accomplish his twofold mission, Hearne found the river, the Coppermine, and followed it to its mouth. It goes without saying that he found no Northwest Passage. Neither did he find any copper, nor interest any new customers. Instead he found the Arctic Ocean, a notable exploit certainly, but of no commercial value of the Hudson's Bay Company.

Company officers were convinced by now that they would have to maintain a permanent post in the heart of the fur country, and they sent Hearne to choose its location and build it. On the lower Saskatchewan he built Cumberland House, the first step in the westward thrust of the Hudson's Bay Company which finally ended at the Pacific Coast. With the building of Cumberland House, the battle between the company and the Montrealers grew increasingly bitter and lawless. It stopped at nothing. Price-cutting, hijacking furs, and debauchery of the Indians became simply more incidents in the course of the day's business.

Such cutthroat competition would in time lead to ruin, especially for the independent traders, who did not control sufficient capital to support a price war. The independents were faced with a dilemma—they must either join forces or go broke. The first independents to combine were Alexander Henry, an American with experience in the Great Lakes trade, and Thomas and Joseph Frobisher, two brothers who had previously operated successfully in the Northwest.

Seeking richer harvests, Henry went north in 1775 with another American, Peter Pond, who was to become a legendary figure in the fur trade. On the Saskatchewan they met and formed a friendship with the Frobishers, and Henry decided to pool his goods with theirs. Pond preferred to trade on his own, but joined them later.

Henry and the Frobishers put in a prosperous winter's trading on the Saskatchewan. The prices they charged their customers were well calculated to make for prosperity. They had no scruples against encouraging trade by selling "English milk," a fanciful Indian name for well-watered traders' rum, and their customers enjoyed many happy sprees, which led to great openhandedness in the disposal of their pelts.

Henry's journal lists these ruinous prices: one made pelt, worth the equivalent of five dollars in Montreal, bought ten musket balls or a half pound of gunpowder; three pelts bought one ax head; ten pelts, one blanket; twenty pelts, one trade musket.

With the coming of spring, the partners went on to the headwaters of the Churchill, one of the rivers that flow to Hudson Bay. Here they met a party of Indians from Lake Athabaska, much farther to the northwest, who were on their way to a Hudson's Bay post at the mouth of the Churchill. After a liberal sampling of the partners' "milk," these Indians were persuaded without great difficulty to go no farther, but to trade their pelts for the fascinating array of luxuries offered here.

Before beginning to transact business, however, they said they were in need of more rum, and made the astonishing request that it be watered, so their young men would not become unmanageable. The rum had already been well watered, but the traders gladly agreed to water it more. Before sampling this second round, the Indians appointed guards whose unwelcome duty it was to stay sufficiently sober to protect their hosts when they indulged in a comparatively mild party, traded their pelts, and went unsteadily on their way home.

After this blatant hijacking of Hudson's Bay Company customers, the partners returned to their base on the Saskatchewan. Other independent traders soon followed their example, pooled their goods, and established a common supply line. The transportation of trade goods to this distant wilderness was so costly that the only way a small partnership of traders could operate successfully was to cooperate with others.

For one of these partnerships, Peter Pond led a trapping party to Lake Athabaska, much farther into the Northwest than any trader had ever ventured. He found so many beavers that he was obliged to leave half his catch to be brought down later. In 1784, a few years after his return to Montreal, Pond took a leading part with Simon McTavish in forming the North West Fur Company, a combine of fur traders that was to grow into the most powerful competitor the Hudson's Bay Company ever met.

Headquarters were established at Montreal with McTavish and Joseph Frobisher, called "agents," in command. The other top officials, known as "wintering partners," were stationed permanently in the wilderness in charge of the various trading posts. They were a remarkable group of men. Hard, canny, often unscrupulous, they formed the backbone of one of the most efficient commercial organizations of all time.

Among "the Nor'westers," a nickname the partners proudly bore, were John McDonald of Garth, six-feet-four-inches tall, with flaming red hair and beard; Roderick McKenzie, who ran a small lending library for his men at his lonely post and devoted his spare time to writing a monumental work on Indian manners and customs; "Big John" McDonnell, called "the priest" because of his piety; Daniel McKenzie, a confirmed friend of the bottle. And Peter Pond, one of the great figures of the Northwest fur trade, a roughhewn, half-literate brawler, but nevertheless a genius. He set up a permanent trading post three thousand water miles from Montreal, Fort Chipewyan, on Lake Athabaska, which he made one of the most productive of all North West Company operations.

Goods from Montreal to supply Fort Chipewyan were not stored at the Grand Portage depot, but were carried to Rainy Lake, much farther west, where a special depot for them was set up, since a round trip between Athabaska and Grand Portage could not be made in one summer. Even to go to Rainy Lake and return, a crew leaving Athabaska as soon as the streams were free of ice had little time for revelry at Rainy. As soon as their pelts were unloaded and a new cargo of supplies taken aboard, they began the return voyage, and were hard put to it to reach home ahead of the fall freeze-up.

At his Athabaska post Peter Pond was the complete despot, his will the only law. His violent character and ungoverned temper led him into frequent quarrels, one of which resulted in a duel that proved fatal to his opponent. About this affair Pond, in his highly imaginative spelling, made this casual entry in his journal: "We met the Next Morning Eairley & Discharged Pistols, in which the Pore Fellowe was Unfortenat." The later murder of a competitor, which Pond was accused of abetting, was too much to accept for even his hard-boiled associates, and they forced him out of the company.

With all his wild and lawless character, Pond was far more than a mere brawling fur trader. He accumulated a vast store of knowledge of the geography of the Northwest country, and inspired Alexander Mackenzie, his second in command, to undertake history-making explorations, one of which led him north from Athabaska to Great Slave Lake and down a long river, now called by his name, to the Arctic Ocean.

After his journey to the Arctic, the sedentary life of a trader palled on Mackenzie. Back at his post on Lake Athabaska, his restless energies demanded more action. Encouraged by Peter Pond, he conceived a great ambition: the discovery of a river route across the continent that would give the North West Company a means of sending furs to the Pacific Coast and shipping them from there to China.

The Pacific Coast of North America was by no means unknown at this time. Russian ships had sailed from Siberia across to Alaska to trade with Indians for the fabulously valuable pelts of the sea otter. Spanish priests from Mexico had established a chain of missions reaching from southern California north to San Francisco Bay. Captain James Cook and Captain George Vancouver, both on voyages of discovery for England, had explored parts of the coast. Both Vancouver and the American merchant skipper Robert Gray had sent their small boats into the Columbia's estuary. The Englishman had judged it to be a bay of the ocean, but one of Gray's boats had cruised well up on the stream in 1792 and recognized it as a river. Gray had named it after his ship, the *Columbia Rediviva*. But only one party of four Spaniards had ever reached the western ocean by marching across the continent.

Added to his ambition to discover for his company a trade route to the Pacific, Mackenzie cherished a personal ambition to be the first man to cross North America. Probably he had never heard of the astonishing transcontinental march of Cabeza de Vaca, member of a Spanish force of four hundred men that sailed from Cuba in 1528 with the object of conquering Florida. Shipwrecked on the peninsula's western coast near Tampa Bay, the would-be conquistadores were so reduced by disease, starvation, and battles with hostile Indians that only Cabeza de Vaca, two soldiers, and a Moorish slave were finally left alive.

After four years of captivity in a local tribe, they escaped and set out afoot for Panuco, a Spanish outpost on the eastern coast of Mexico, which they expected to reach in a few days' march. They did not reach it in a few days, nor did they ever reach it.

Month after month they kept going west, ceremoniously escorted from tribe to tribe by natives who believed them to be gods. After more than two years of wandering, during which they had collected some six hundred worshipful followers, the four exiles met a gang of Spanish slave hunters who guided them to Culiacán, a nearby Spanish outpost on the Gulf of California, some two thousand miles west of where their march had started.

From Lake Athabaska, Alexander Mackenzie, aged thirty, started on his journey across the continent in the spring of 1793.

In his party were Alexander Mackay, his clerk, six *voyageurs*, two Indians, and a dog. Their twenty-five-foot birchbark canoe, with its load of presents for the Indians and supplies for themselves, weighed three thousand pounds.

Thanks to Peter Pond's and his own geographical knowledge, Mackenzie knew that two great river routes led out of Lake Athabaska, one of which he had already explored. It had carried him to Great Slave Lake and on to the Arctic Ocean.

The other route, the Peace River, flowed into Athabaska from the west. This he would try. If he had known what was in store for him, even his magnificent courage might have faltered. Like every other geographer of his time, Mackenzie believed the continent was much narrower than it is, and he had no conception of a tremendous barrier running north and south from Mexico to the Arctic. The Rocky Mountains were not yet on the map. He believed that headwaters of rivers flowing eastward surely must interlock, or at least closely approach, headwaters of those flowing to the Pacific. A short portage over "the height of land" was all he expected.

After many twists and turns, but making generally to the west, the Peace River carried Mackenzie's canoe to its headwaters in the Rockies. The first formidable challenge of the mountains was Peace River Canyon, a deep gorge through which tumbled twenty miles of roaring white water. It took the party nearly a week to tow their boat by hand lines through this gorge and carry the baggage along the base of its towering walls. Beyond the canyon, they struggled westward for many heartbreaking days among tremendous ranges, forcing their canoe through stretch after stretch of wild rapids.

In north central British Columbia, where the Finlay and Parsnip Rivers join to form the Peace, Mackenzie turned south to ascend the Parsnip, as he had been advised to do by an old Indian. After forcing his way up many miles of rapids on the Parsnip, he found a carrying place that the old Indian had told him to take. A portage of only half a mile led to a river that we know as the Fraser, which flows to the Pacific. The party had crossed the Continental Divide.

Explorer Alexander Mackenzie, along with his clerk, six "voyageurs," two Indians and a dog, started on a journey across the continent in the spring of 1793.

At Prince George Canyon on the Fraser, Mackenzie was told that he could neither get through in a canoe nor walk along the banks. His Indian informers said that in going farther west they always used a long overland trail that left the river some miles upstream from where they now were. At this news the men were on the point of mutiny and begged Mackenzie to give up and start home. But he was too near victory to think of surrender, and his determination to go on won them over.

After first building a new canoe to replace their badly battered old one, they grudgingly turned back up the Fraser. When the trail that the Indians had described was found, they hid the canoe, made packs of a part of their supplies, and went on afoot over a rough mountain path that finally led them down to a village of the Bellacoola Indians. Among these slovenly but friendly people they found many manufactured articles, sure evidence that the ocean was not far away.

The Bellacoolas agreed to take Mackenzie on to the sea in one of their big wooden canoes, and they all happily embarked on the little river that ran by the village. On the way, when the Indians went ashore for a short visit with friends, Mackenzie's little dog, the companion of all their trials, mysteriously disappeared. Regretfully, they went on without him. On July 20, 1793, sixty-eight days after the start from Lake Athabaska, the first men since Cabeza de Vaca to cross the continent of North America glided out of the Bella Coola River into Dean Channel, a narrow bay which soon led them to the Pacific Coast northeast of Vancouver Island.

They did not tarry long. The Indians here were too familiar with the ways of white sailors to trust their visitors, and were not only inhospitable, but surly and threatening. By crude pantomime, one of them made the Canadians understand that he had recently been attacked by "Macubah and Bensins," two men from a ship cruising offshore, and he proposed to avenge the insult by removing Mackenzie. That master of Indian diplomacy succeeded in sweetening the heart of his assailant with gifts, but he was greatly puzzled to know who had planted in this savage such deadly thirst for vengeance.

The faded pages of an old logbook, kept by the captain of a ship that had cruised these waters shortly before Mackenzie's arrival, gives the answer. If the man who had fought his way across a thousand miles of trackless wilderness had reached the coast six weeks earlier, he would have been astonished to find in Dean Channel several small boats manned by English sailors. They were making soundings for His Britannic Majesty's ship *Discovery*, on a voyage of exploration for the British navy. "Macubah" and "Bensins" were Captain George Vancouver, her master, and his naturalist, Archibald Menzies.

On his return up the river, Mackenzie was delighted to be greeted enthusiastically by his lost dog at the Bellacoola village. However, when he reached Montreal, he was nettled by the lack of enthusiasm for his exploit on the part of his fellow Nor'westers. The company could greatly profit by a waterway to the Pacific, of course, but what the partners wanted was a fulfillment of the old dream: a wide, deep passage across the continent, through which seagoing ships could sail their unobstructed way from the Atlantic to the Pacific. Of what use for shipping tons and tons of beaver was an endless succession of small lakes, tumultuous rivers, and mountainous overland carries?

Mackenzie himself was well aware of the commercial importance of his discoveries. He had found a path to the western ocean, a rough one, to be sure, but he was convinced that smoother ones existed and could be found. His associates saw only the immediate difficulties. They were content to go on with the present volume of business, which, to his wider vision, was picayune compared to what it might become.

In disgust he quit the North West Company and went to London, where he was lionized by society and knighted by King George III. Hoping to influence the British ministry, he wrote a widely read book, *Voyages from Montreal*, about his travels. It outlined clearly his plans for reorganizing the American fur trade on a truly continental scale, and emphasized the importance of gaining control of the western coast before it could be occupied by the infant American republic. He believed that the Fraser, the big river he had quit to begin the portage to the Bellacoolas, was the great river of the west, the Columbia. "With its mouth included in the British holdings," he wrote, "the entire command of the fur trade of North America might be obtained."

Mackenzie's book, which gave plain warning that the British were casting envious eyes on the Pacific Coast, was read with great interest by a man who had been thinking along similar lines, but from the viewpoint of a citizen of another country. This was Thomas Jefferson, newly elected President of the United States, who had gone on from thinking of his country as a narrow strip of colonies along the Atlantic Coast to visions of it as a great continent-spanning nation.

The influence of the beaver on the course of international rivalry was growing apace. The need of the British fur companies for new trapping grounds had led them from Hudson Bay across the continent, and had brought them into direct competition with the interests of the United States.

Grand Portage

Where the border between Minnesota and Ontario ends at Lake Superior, the shoreline is dented by a lovely little bay, still unspoiled by the "progress" that has marred so many of our country's beauty spots. During the last decade of the eighteenth century, this was one of the most important centers in the Canadian fur country. Here in July of every summer the surrounding hills echoed the raucous revelry of a thousand beaver trappers, *voyageurs*, and Indians, gathered for the annual rendezvous of the North West Fur Company.

On the shore of this bay was located the field headquarters of the company, a large, palisaded fort which surrounded storehouses, living quarters, mess hall, powder magazine, trading house, and council hall. Over all flew the British ensign. An ancient Indian trail led westward from this post to beyond the great falls of Pigeon River, the beginning of the Northwest Road. This trail was the Grand Portage—nine miles uphill and downhill over a rough, muddy footpath. "Like the road to heaven," said the *voyageurs*, "narrow, beset with thorns and muskegs." Every greenhorn, on his first trip over this portage, was obliged to submit to initiation ceremonies, like a sailor on first crossing the equator. After being thoroughly doused with buckets of water, he solemnly swore to observe certain obligations, one of which was a promise never to kiss the wife of a fellow *voyageur* without her freely given consent.

This was the ancient gate to the Northwest country, known to Indians from time immemorial. Here, and only here, a man could find a gap through the rugged cliffs that border the northwest shore of Lake Superior and go on by river, lake, and portage far into the trackless country beyond. By going through this gap he could reach the headwaters of the Mississippi, or go wherever else his desires might lead him. Here both Duluth, "captain of the *coureurs de bois*," and Pierre La Vérendrye, former commander for the French in this region, had maintained trading posts long ago. It continued to be the principal wilderness post of the company until 1803, when the land on which it stood was ceded to the United States. Then it was supplanted by Fort William, only thirty miles away, but within British territory.

At rendezvous time, hundreds of Indians erected their rude bark wigwams along the shore of the bay at Grand Portage. They came here to barter their pelts and to enjoy a short celebration, for strong drink was always in good supply. Those who were short of pelts brought live merchandise: their squaws and daughters. At the rear of the fort, tents were pitched to shelter the hundreds of *voyageurs*, trappers, and traders who had come from Montreal and from the north country.

Supplies to be distributed from Grand Portage to the up-country posts were brought from Montreal in big birchbark canoes called *canots du maître*, thirty-five to forty feet long and six feet wide amidships. Each canoe weighed around five hundred pounds and required a crew of eight to ten men. A full cargo, with the crew, sank the gunwales to within six inches of the water. These boats were so tippy that it was a hackneyed joke that the crews found it necessary to part their hair in the middle.

The *voyageurs* who manned the smaller *canots du nord* of the country beyond Grand Portage considered themselves the aristocrats of the trade. They looked down their noses at the crews of the *canots du maître*, whom they contemptuously dubbed "pork eaters," because of their hominy and melted lard rations. This low rating was entirely unjustified. The pork eaters, with superb skill and courage, paddled, pushed, towed, and carried their big boats over the perilous thousand-mile run from Montreal to Grand Portage, a journey that would have broken both the backs and hearts of lesser men.

At the Grand Portage storehouse, the supplies they brought from Montreal were rearranged in ninety-pound packs to suit requirements of the various up-country posts, then carried, two packs to a man, across the nine-mile trail. The load rested on the carrier's back, supported by a tumpline—a long leather strap fastened at either end to the packs, with its broad middle part resting against his forehead. At the other end of the portage, the packs were stowed in the smaller north-country canoes, which had brought down packs of made pelts from their far-flung bases. A good man might make a round trip over the portage in six hours—eighteen miles of hard slogging, half that distance with a load of a hundred and eighty pounds on his back.

The up-country crews carried their packs of pelts in the opposite direction over the portage to the shore of Lake Superior, where they were stowed in the *canots du maître* for the return journey to Montreal. As aristocrats passed pork eaters along the trail, lusty sallies and good-natured insults were flung from one to another, which sometimes led to fisticuffs later at the canteen.

Not before this work was behind him could the *voyageur* don his holiday finery, draw his pay—or borrow on next year's pay—and devote himself to less arduous diversions. At the canteen, rum and the Indian girls usually got it all before he again set out with empty pockets and light heart for Montreal or the north country.

At rendezvous time every summer, the partners of the North West Company gathered at Grand Portage for their annual meeting. At the end of his long journey from Montreal, Simon Mc-Tavish, the *"premier,"* was carried ashore in great state on the shoulders of his canoe men amid the welcoming greetings of his associates. All the wintering partners who could possibly get away from their posts came to sit with him around the long, felt-covered table in the council hall, where they listened to his Jovian pronouncements and shrewd plans for next season's business. They sincerely admired McTavish as a man and greatly respected his judgment. Outside the council hall pandemonium might reign, but the partners always had serious business of the company to consider, and they considered it thoughtfully and wisely.

The climax of the rendezvous came with a grand fling on the last night—a ball at which everybody danced enthusiastically until dawn. The partners attended, dressed in their most formal bib and tucker, complete with swords. Clerks, bookkeepers, the staff who were accorded the title "gentleman" were there, somewhat tipsy, perhaps, but all striving to live up to the title.

The most personable of the squaws were invited—chieftains were likely to imbibe too much firewater to be an addition. The Indian women were apt pupils at learning the reels and jigs that were danced to the music of one or two fiddles, to which might be added a flute or the bagpipes. If there were not enough squaws to go around, the men danced together with almost equal fervor. Occasional fistfights provided an added element of excitement to these affairs. An entry in the diary of one participant reads, "Finally two battles were fought, which put an end to this truly genteel Northwestern ball."

Outside the hall another party, even more uninhibited, was in progress at the same time. The canoe hands, both aristocrats and pork eaters, joined with the Indians in one last frenzied jamboree. Yells, shrill laughter, and agonized shrieks mingled with gunshots, drumbeats, and war cries, all to the accompaniment of the bawling of terrified papooses and the howling of innumerable dogs. This was not a mutual massacre of Indians and whites. It was merely a celebration to mark the breakup of the rendezvous. This was no party for gentlemen, but it was greatly enjoyed by those who took part.

In the early gloom of the next morning, the revelers started home to recuperate and look forward to next year's "genteel" party.

The Daily Life
of a Wintering Partner

The wintering partners of the North West Company made their way far into the virgin territory beyond Lake Superior, establishing trading posts as far north as Lake Athabaska, westward to the Rocky Mountains, and eventually to the Pacific Ocean.

The life of a Nor'wester in this bleak, lonely country was no life for a weakling. At his headquarters in an isolated wilderness fort, the *bourgeois* of a post waged an unending struggle against weather, starvation, his unstable employees, and his savage neighbors. It was necessary for him to cultivate the good will of the Indians, on whom he must depend to trap most of his beaver. As a result of the white man's own vicious trading practices, the adherence of the fickle savages could be held only by frequent doles of hard liquor, and that nearly always led to fighting and bloodshed. The Indians trapped partly to get pelts to exchange for pots and kettles, but their chief spur had come to be the anticipation of a spree. If they could not look forward to a spree anywhere, they did not bother to trap.

Many a post commander recognized that the debauching of the Indians was a great evil, but his competitor sold rum, and unless he sold it too he had no trade. Trade was his business; the welfare of the Indian, he reasoned, was no concern of his.

Final authority in these widely scattered forts was exercised by the *bourgeois*, usually a partner in the company, who was responsible to headquarters in Montreal for a profitable return of pelts each summer. He must be an able administrator as well as a man of powerful, dominating personality in order to control the residents of his post and his customers. He led an arduous, lonely life, relieved only by the excitement of danger.

We can form a vivid picture of such a life from the journal of a man who lived it for many years and kept a written record of his experiences from day to day. He was called Alexander Henry the Younger, to distinguish him from his uncle of the same name, whom we have previously met as a partner of the Frobisher brothers. The younger Henry served for many years as *bourgeois* of trading posts that he established in the northeast corner of the present state of North Dakota. His first post stood on Park River, a little above its junction with the Red River of the North. Later he

built another post some thirty-five miles north on the Red River at
the mouth of the Pembina. His stockaded forts were situated at the
edge of the great eastern Canadian forests. Rolling prairies, grazing ground of countless herds of buffalo, stretched westward to the
Rocky Mountains. Henry's trapping territory lay along the
future border between Canada and the United States. At his time,
no border line had been established, and both countries claimed the
area.

Alexander Henry's diary, begun when he was a clerk in the
company's service, runs almost without interruption from 1799 to
1814. It ends in an unfinished sentence on the night before his
death.

During this time he lived to its fullest the life of a typical
Nor'wester *bourgeois*. He was no better, nor was he any worse,
than others of his kind. He debauched the Indians with rum to oil
the wheels of trade, then bound up the wounds they suffered in the
resulting drunken brawls. He doctored their minor and major ills
in a crude way, cajoled them, fought with them, and married
"after the fashion of the country" one of their women. Among a
clan of renowned tipplers, he was one of the most notable, but he
was no drunkard; he was always self-controlled and confined his
indulgence to appropriate times and places. He was in all respects a
typical hard-living, hard-driving *bourgeois*, but he had a lighter
side too. He was an enthusiastic gardener, a keen observer, appre-
ciative of the beauties of the country, genuinely interested in its
people and its animal life. He compiled a vocabulary giving the
equivalents of 330 English words in four Indian languages. His
diary never fails to note the first birds to arrive in spring, nor to
express wonder at the migrating flights of swans, geese, and the
tremendous flocks of passenger pigeons, so dense that they blotted
out the sun. He is amazed at the vast herds of buffalo, and notes the
preference shown by female wolves in heat for his domestic male
dogs.

Like Samuel Pepys, the famous English diarist, Henry set
down his daily doings, whether important or trivial, with remarkable frankness and without comment as to their ethics. He writes of

grievous suffering and gruesome horrors in the most forthright way, merely stating the facts as they occurred. His infrequent censure is confined to business rivals and to a few particularly obnoxious Indians.

One of the most annoying characters among the residents of his Pembina post was an old chief named Tabashaw, who repeatedly tried to murder him and constantly bred mischief among his people. Henry's undoubted aversion for all Indians is expressed in his diary only by inference. References to Tabashaw always show plainly that Henry considered him a vicious old reprobate. One entry reads: "Indians drinking at the fort. Tabashaw stabbed a near relative in six different places in the breast and sides; every stab went up to the handle. The poor fellow lingered an hour and died." He at length records with ironic satisfaction the death of "our great chief Tabashaw" at the hands of the Sioux.

From long experience Henry knew that an Indian drinking party was sure to lead to fighting and often to murder, but he persistently sold rum in exchange for beaver. Occasionally he set it up on the house as a reward for good hunting, or to wash grief from the heart of a sorrowing widower, or merely because his customers felt an overweening yearning for a spree.

Such calculated enticement to retain the allegiance of customers, common to all Nor'wester posts, was not wholly approved by Henry, as is shown by an entry in which he indulges in a bit of soul-searching: "The Indians totally neglect their ancient customs. And to what can this degeneracy be ascribed but to their intercourse with us, to teach them roguery and destroy both mind and body with that pernicious article rum? What a different set of people they would be were there not a drop of liquor in the country!"

The rum of the fur trade was not actually rum at all. It was concentrated alcohol, called "high wine," diluted with as much water as the traffic would bear. For tribes unaccustomed to this violent beverage, four or five quarts of high wine were mixed with nine gallons of water; for more experienced topers, from six to as many as nine quarts of high wine in nine gallons of water were necessary to produce a satisfied customer. To the simple savage with no built-up resistance to alcohol, this concoction was rank poison that led to all sorts of mad excesses. If the party grew unmanageable, a generous dose of knockout drops in the form of laudanum was added to the mixture. Little Shell, a particularly seasoned drinker, seemed to be immune to the effect of laudanum. On one occasion six doses of twenty drops each, administered within an hour, failed to put a damper on his enthusiasm.

For the Indian, rum was an expensive luxury. At Henry's post on Park River, a spoonful or two of high wine mixed with a quart of water cost the buyer five or six prime beaver pelts. One of Henry's traders, in charge of an outpost, bought 120 beaver skins for eight quarts of rum, two blankets, and a pocket mirror. Rated at wilderness prices, these articles stood the trader about thirty dollars. The pelts were sold at Montreal for four hundred dollars.

Entirely without emotion, our diarist records dreadful atrocities inflicted by Indians upon one another as a result of imbibing his wares: "Grand Guelle stabbed Perdrix Blanche with a knife in six places. The latter, in fighting with his wife, fell in the fire and was almost roasted, but had strength enough left, notwithstanding his wounds, to bite her nose off. He is very ill, but I don't suppose he will die."

Biting off the end of the nose was a common Indian way of expressing disapproval of the conduct of a faithless wife. Henry mentions one such case in which the severed part fell into the snow and disappeared. After an intensive search, the now regretful husband found it and bound it back into its accustomed position.

But Henry's life was not by any means a constant succession of such sordid incidents. Every summer he made the long journey to Grand Portage to take part in the yearly meeting of the Nor'-westers. On these trips, if his convoy happened to encounter a convoy from another of the company's posts, an exciting race was sure to follow. Henry was a popular man among his partners, friendly and outgoing, and after long months with no companions but Indians he delighted in the company of men of his own kind who joined him at the yearly festivities.

From his headquarters at Pembina, Henry made frequent visits to his outposts in the Hair Hills and other places where he kept small crews of trappers permanently stationed. In winter these journeys could be dangerous, and he had many narrow escapes from death by blizzards, starvation, or at the hands of hostile Indians.

The tribes with whom he traded were Chippewas, Crees, and Assiniboins, reasonably friendly as a rule, but always fickle and uncertain. He had to be constantly wary of them, especially when they were intoxicated. The Sioux, their deadly enemies, seemed always to be on the prowl in search of scalps. The slightest unusual occurrence at the post—the squawk of an unknown bird, the glimpse of an elk seen dimly through the forest, somebody's dream that the Sioux were coming, a cloud of smoke on the horizon —anything was enough to start a panic, with screaming squaws clutching their children and dashing for the fort, and bucks running around in circles shooting bullets at the sky.

Each spring Henry planted a garden, and the rich soil produced magnificent vegetables for his table. Pride in the result of his gardening efforts is evident: "I measured an onion twenty-two inches in circumference; a carrot eighteen inches long, and at the thick end, fourteen inches in circumference; a turnip with its leaves weighed twenty-five pounds, and the leaves alone weighed fifteen pounds." He did not always have such success, however. Raids on the garden by Indian neighbors were frequent in spite of its being closely guarded.

In the fall of 1807, an entry reads: "Swarms of grasshoppers have destroyed the greater part of the vegetables in my kitchen garden. . . . The swarms appear about the 15th of June, generally in clouds from the south, and spread destruction; the very trees are stripped of their leaves. Grasshoppers pass northward until millions are drowned in Lake Winnipeg and cause a horrid stench." At times the quiet satisfaction of husbandry was marred by "disagreeable incidents." For example: "Indians having asked for liquor and promised to decamp and hunt well all summer, I gave them some. Grand Guelle stabbed Capot Rouge, Le Boeur stabbed his young wife in the arm, Little Shell almost beat his old mother's brains out with a club, and there was terrible fighting among them. I sowed garden seeds.''

Henry was always in a state of wonder at the wealth of animal life around him. "No noise is heard but that of swans and geese screaming as they fly on their way to warmer climates. . . . Wolves are very numerous; they go in large droves, and keep up a terrible howling day and night." During their rutting time, the bellowing of the buffalo bulls kept him awake at night. The vast herds were almost beyond belief.

> *At daybreak I was awakened by the bellowing of the buffaloes. I got up and was astonished when I climbed into the southwest bastion. On my right the plains were black and appeared as if in motion, south to north. Opposite the fort the ice was covered, and on my left, to the utmost extent of the reach below us, the river was covered with buffalo moving northward. . . . I had seen almost incredible numbers in the fall, but nothing in comparison with what I now beheld. The ground was covered at every point of the compass as far as the eye could reach, and every animal was in motion.*

And the next day, "the plains were still covered with buffalo, moving slowly northward."

In spring as the ice on the river began to soften, thousands of the heavy beasts would break through. An entry at the end of March reads: "Rain broke up the ice; it drifted in large masses, making a great noise by crushing, tumbling, and tossing in every direction, driven by a strong current. It continued to drift on the 31st, bearing great numbers of dead buffalo from above, which must have been drowned in attempting to cross while the ice was weak." Next day: "The river is clear of ice, but entire herds of drowned buffalo continue to drift by. Several are lodged on the bank near the fort. The women cut up some of the fattest for their own use; the flesh appeared to be fresh and good. It really is astonishing what vast numbers have perished; they formed one continuous line in the current for two days and nights."

The melancholy procession did not cease even then. In an entry of two weeks later we read, "Drowned buffalo still drifting down the river, but not in such vast numbers as before." The stench became well nigh intolerable to Henry, but the Indians suffered no discomfort—they liked buffalo meat best after it had begun to spoil.

John Macdonnell, another Nor'wester, cruising the Qu'Appelle River late in May, counted the buffalo carcasses he passed in one day's descent of the river. His count totaled 7,360. Great fires swept the prairie every spring. Macdonnell writes: "Blind buffalo seen every moment wandering about. The poor beasts have all the hair singed off them, and their eyes are swollen and closed fast. It was really pitiful to see them staggering about, sometimes running afoul of a large stone, at other times tumbling down hill and falling into creeks."

Henry kept a pet bear which he had raised from a cub. It was perfectly tame and a great friend of the dogs, who welcomed it as a companion. In late fall he writes: "My tame bear making a hole, apparently desirous of taking up winter quarters. I got a place made for him, but he did not like it; although snug and warm, he preferred making a place for himself."

Wild bears were numerous, both grizzlies and blacks. At one time Henry saw seven drinking together out of the same pool. He writes: "Bears make prodigious ravages in the brush and willows; the plum trees are torn to pieces and every tree that bears fruit has shared the same fate. The tops of the oaks are also very roughly handled, broken and torn down to get the acorns."

Bear meat was passable as food, and the furred skins made warm bed robes, but it was the fat that was especially prized. Melted down and poured into bags made of buffalo hide, it kept sweet for months and was good for eating in chunks, for seasoning, and for making pemmican. The Indians used it as a foundation cream for face paint, to anoint their hair, and as a body ointment to give them a bear's ferocity—and an odor that announced their presence at a considerable distance.

In addition to buffalo and bear, there were many other species

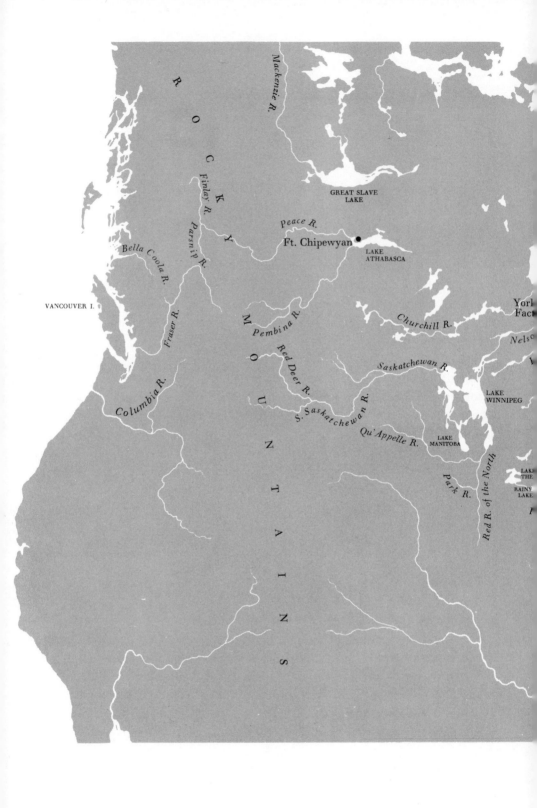

*French Canada, the Hudson
Bay and the great Northwest.*

of game: moose, deer, elk, and great flights of wild fowl. Flocks of passenger pigeons, a bird that is now extinct, darkened the sky for several days at a time. Henry delighted in hunting and spent many happy hours running buffalo on horseback over the prairie, and ranging the woods with his fowling piece. The rivers teemed with fish, from great sturgeon weighing up to 150 pounds down to the much smaller but delicious whitefish.

It is difficult to conceive that anyone could ever lack food with such an abundance of game at hand, yet we find numerous references to cases of near starvation in the journals kept at various posts. Due to Alexander Henry's foresightedness, Pembina's icehouse seldom lacked a generous supply of meat and fish. There were green vegetables in season, and potatoes could be kept through the year.

But in some Nor'west posts, beyond the range of the buffalo and where other game might be lacking in winter, the near approach of starvation is frequently evidenced by such entries in post journals as: "We were reduced to eating the parchment out of our windows"; "We dined on a pair of leather breeches"; "We were obliged to take the hair from the bearskins and roast the hide, which tastes like pork." And as an example of living on capital, "We destroyed, in order to keep alive, upward of three hundred beaver skins, besides a few lynx and otter skins. We have a meal now and then; at intervals we are still two or three days without anything." One journal tells of the men living for a time on rosebuds, "a kind of food neither very palatable nor nourishing."

Posts that were located in buffalo country had scant need to resort to such bizarre food. By all accounts, the steaks and chops from a fat buffalo cow made very superior eating. The tongue and hump were regarded as especial delicacies, as were also beaver tails and moose snouts. The Indians relished roasted dog—a food that found little favor with Alexander Henry, although his half-breed trappers did not spurn it. Buffalo fat was highly useful. Melted down and stored in rawhide bags, called *taureaux*, it would keep sweet indefinitely. It was chiefly used for making pemmican, an Indian dish that was the staple food for long marches and canoe voyages. Pemmican could be eaten as it came from the bag, or boiled with corn or wild rice to make a sort of stew, called "rubba-boo." Two pounds of pemmican per day would sustain a man, where the normal daily ration of fresh meat was eight pounds.

The principal ingredient of pemmican was the lean, fleshy parts of either buffalo or beaver. Well dried and smoked, the meat was pounded to a pulp and mixed with fat—forty pounds of fat to fifty pounds of meat. For fastidious diners, dried berries or maple sugar were sometimes added. Stored in bags each holding ninety pounds, this made a palatable and nourishing food that would keep fresh over a long period.

At a few posts within the buffalo range, the making of pemmican was the principal business, and their product was distributed throughout the trapping country. For the winterbound trapper in the northern wilderness, it was the staff of life.

When beaver-trapping was slack at Pembina in midwinter, Henry's men amused themselves by sliding on sleds down the hill leading to the river from the south gate of the fort. "Their descent is so great as to cause their trains to run across the Red River. The women join them and they have excellent sport." The squaws played a favorite game on the ice, called *coullion*, while the more dignified bucks sat around the fires in their wigwams "at their favorite game of platter, and others beat the drum and sing their wabeno songs. . . . The dogs have fine sport chasing the old bulls that take shelter in the woods, but they are very alert and active for animals of their bulk and the dogs cannot hurt them."

In summer there were the usual agonizing myriads of mosquitoes. With the first hint of winter, legions of mice deserted the outdoors to invade the warm living quarters, destroying everything they could gnaw, riddling blankets, even carrying off the colored beads that were a staple article of trade. Not in the least shy, they played on Henry's bed and scampered over his face as he tried to sleep. A cat donated by the *bourgeois* of another post took care of this situation.

The Indians were an extremely noisy lot. Conversation, especially among the women, was carried on mainly in loud shouts punctuated by shrill bursts of laughter. Any death was the occasion of days and nights of exaggerated mourning by relatives, expressed by constant shrieks and moans that nearly drove Henry mad. Witch doctors carried on their professional practice by beating drums, and shaking rattles, along with thunderous bellowing. This was all designed to scare away the evil spirit that had caused whatever ailed the patient. Henry frequently took to the prairies to get away from the din.

It was a rare Nor'wester who denied himself the comfort of a female companion to share his quarters, cook his meals, and mend his clothes. Alexander Henry was no exception. After a riotous New Year's celebration at the post on Park River, he went to his quarters in the gray morning hours to find them already occupied.

His entry of January 1, 1801, reads, "Laird's daughter took possession of my room, and the devil himself could not have got her out." Next morning, on being met with a firm refusal when he urged her to return to her father's hut, he went out to hunt buffalo. On his return from the chase he notes, "I was vexed to find my room still occupied, and no sign of her budging." At the end of a month, she still had not budged. On January 30 he sounds a hopeful note: "I got rid of my bed-fellow, who returned to her father with good grace. Fine weather." But two days later, hope was supplanted by resignation. "The lady returned. A terrible snowstorm." After this there appears now and then a casual mention of "Her Ladyship" in the diary.

This is the extent of Henry's revelation of his romance, but the lady's persistence evidently overcame his reluctance to accept the responsibilities of a family man. Ten years later the roster of Fort Vermillion, a post on the North Saskatchewan where he was stationed, lists the occupants of his apartment as "Self . . . 1 man— 1 woman—3 children."

Amid these distractions, Henry never lost sight of the fact that his principal business was the collection of beaver pelts. His chief reliance for trapping was a band of some fifty Indians who lived in their village beside his fort. In addition, several outlying posts,

operated by subordinates, traded with roving bands in their neigh-
borhoods. At intervals during the winter, he visited these outposts
to satisfy himself that the men were trapping industriously, to
collect their beaver pelts, or to compose their frequent quarrels.

The return of pelts from Pembina was not impressive compared
to some of the larger Nor'west posts, but Henry always did a fair
amount of business. During his best seasons, the annual catch
amounted to around eighteen hundred skins. The annual total
return for all North West Company posts averaged about eighty
thousand skins.

The Indian or half-breed hunter took to the woods in the fall,
when fur began to grow long, dense, dark in color. His outfit—
ammunition, weapons, and other necessities—was advanced to him
on credit at the beginning of the season. This was his debt, to be
repaid in pelts when he turned in his catch.

During the cold winter, fur reached its prime. With the earliest
hint of spring, the life of the beaver became a series of tragedies. At
any moment he might be caught in one of the clumsy iron traps
made by blacksmiths. In the absence of traps, the walls of his lodge
might be chopped through or his dam destroyed to drain the pond,
and the bewildered animal killed with a club or ax as he tried to
escape. It was a cruel, bloody business, but fashionable gentlemen
in Europe must have their beaver hats, and were willing to pay for
them.

It was considered a shrewd stroke to go into the woods and
persuade another company's hunter to sell his furs to you. Both
the Hudson's Bay Company and the XY Company of Montreal
maintained posts near Pembina, and the scramble for pelts among
the three was always fierce and ruthless. Nor'westers grudgingly
respected the Hudson's Bay Company, whom they derisively
called "the Potties."

At Pembina, trading with Indians was conducted with ceremony and decorum—until the rum began to take effect. A party
of hunters fresh from the woods fired a salute on reaching the post,
to which it responded by raising the British flag. Then they
checked their weapons at the gate and entered the stockade. After

ceremonial smoking and several long-winded orations, a round of drinks was served on the house. With the customers' appetites whetted by this largesse, the meeting was in proper shape to start doing business. This was no bargain sale, as is shown by a typical scale of Pembina prices. Thirty beaver skins bought a keg of liquor; fourteen skins, a gun; six, a blanket; two, an ax; three, a fathom of Brazil tobacco. A scalping knife, as distinguished from the more widely useful hunting knife, could be purchased for one skin.

So much for the day-to-day life of a Nor'wester *bourgeois*. A man with a taste for adventure and an appreciation of wild country and primitive people might come to love such a life—and there were many who did love it. Alexander Henry the Younger was one of these. In spite, or perhaps because, of the many difficulties and perils of his calling, he followed it to the end of his days.

IV

UP THE MISSOURI
AND ACROSS THE ROCKIES

Revolution and Real Estate Deal

IN THE SUMMER OF 1776, TWO FUR TRADERS SET
out for Grand Portage from their base on the Saskatchewan to lay
in next year's supply of trade goods. On the way they stopped at
Lake of the Woods, where one of them, Alexander Henry the
Elder, made a puzzled entry in his diary. "Indians," he wrote,
"have spread a rumor that some strange nation has entered Montreal, taken Quebec, and will certainly be at Grand Portage before
we arrive there." Though somewhat exaggerated, this rumor was
founded on fact. It was a garbled account of the unsuccessful attempt of an army from New England to invade Canada. The
American Revolution had begun.

The events of the war that brought about the birth of the United
States of America have no real bearing on our story, but its
results, as they affected the fur industry, do concern us.

Both France and Spain were involved on the side of the colonials,
France as an active ally and Spain as a source of military supplies.
Neither of these nations was prompted to participate by any deep-
seated sympathy for the American cause, but rather by the
determination of both to curb England's ambitions in North
America. The Treaty of Paris that ended the war recognized the
independence of the thirteen American colonies, left England in
possession of Canada, and Spain master of Florida and Louisiana.
The western boundary of the new United States was fixed at the
Mississippi, but nobody knew the western limits of Canada and
Louisiana.

The Canadians held that their territory extended westward to the Pacific. Its boundary with the thirteen colonies was fixed as following the old *voyageur* route, the Northwest Road, from Lake Superior to Lake of the Woods, and from there due west to the Mississippi—an impossibility, because such a line would pass north of any headwater of that river. Louisiana had been declared by La Salle to include all the lands drained by the Mississippi and its tributaries, but the treaty transferred the Mississippi drainage east of the river to the United States. The western limits of Louisiana, as La Salle has defined them, fell far short of being a definite boundary.

The discontent that had sparked the rebellion of the thirteen colonies had never extended to Canada. There the economy had always been founded on the fur trade, as it had been founded on agriculture farther south along the Atlantic Coast. Settlement of the Canadian West by homesteaders was not desired by the fur interests, for that would mean an end of beaver-trapping.

The great fur companies were the controlling financial powers of Canada, and most of the population was dependent on them for a living. The prosperity of the people depended upon the prosperity of the fur companies and the interests of both determined their loyalty to England. Parliament had ruled that all Canadian territory north of the Ohio was closed to settlers. That area was to remain forever a wilderness, a hunting ground for trappers and a perpetual breeding ground for beavers. This was as the fur interests would have it.

So here again the lowly rodent had influenced the course of great events by keeping the Canadians loyal to England, while the farmers of the English colonies farther south broke their ties with the mother country.

The new American republic now occupied only that part of the continent lying between the Atlantic Coast and the Mississippi River. No conception of a continent-wide empire had ever been a part of the national thinking. But the third man elected to the Presidency came to the office in 1801 with a wider view. Thomas Jefferson had long foreseen the expansion of the republic westward, and he had scarcely been installed in office before he laid plans for a look beyond the Mississippi.

By this time, a conqueror of overweening ambition and un-exampled genius had come to power in France, and had begun to shift the nations of Europe about as if they were pawns on a chessboard. Napoleon Bonaparte, in a secret treaty with the Spanish king, had repossessed for France her lost territory of Louisiana. Spain, granted Louisiana in 1763 by the Treaty of Paris, no longer wanted the colony, which for years had cost her more than it had returned in revenues. Napoleon offered to give Spain territory that he intended to conquer in northern Italy and promised to maintain Louisiana permanently as a buffer between the United States and Spanish Mexico. As he planned it, Louisiana would be the foundation of a new French empire in North America which would eventually become powerful enough to drive England from the continent, and perhaps destroy the upstart American republic.

As a first step to put this scheme into effect, Napoleon sent a force to conquer the island of Santo Domingo, and prepared to occupy Louisiana with an army of ten thousand men. Yellow fever and guerrilla warfare destroyed his army in Santo Domingo, and he lost interest in Louisiana.

The Spanish authorities at New Orleans, as yet unaware of the secret transfer of Louisiana to Napoleon and still in control of the province, arbitrarily closed the Mississippi to American commerce, causing a tremendous uproar among the fur interests up the river.

In an attempt to cure this situation, Jefferson sent commissioners to Paris with authority to make Napoleon a cash offer for New Orleans and a part of Florida. After a period of haggling, the American commissioners were astonished one day to be asked if their government would be interested in purchasing the entire province of Louisiana! Napoleon had reneged on his promise to Spain and was willing to sell. The American commissioners were indeed interested. By the gargantuan real estate deal that resulted, the western boundary of the American republic leaped from the

Mississippi to the Rocky Mountains. The United States of America had more than doubled its area, a fact that was only dimly realized at the time. The cost of Louisiana, including interest, amounted to more than $23,000,000, or about four cents an acre.

On the ninth of March, 1804, the citizens of the frontier town of St. Louis assembled in front of Government House. The Spanish ensign was lowered and the tricolor of France floated momentarily in its place as the cannons of the old fort roared a salute. The tricolor was then lowered and the Stars and Stripes run up. A detachment of the U.S. army that had marched from Cahokia, on the opposite side of the river, presented arms, and documents were signed that acknowledged the sovereignty of the United States over Louisiana.

By far the greater part of this area was unexplored wilderness, and the first concern of the new owners was to learn something about the trackless domain that they had bought sight unseen. One of the signers of the documents at the transfer ceremony was a young captain of the First U.S. Infantry who had come from his camp a few miles upriver. He was present as the personal representative of the President of the United States. More than a year previously he had been ordered by Jefferson to organize and lead a small expedition up the Missouri and seek out a route from its headwaters to the Pacific Ocean. This was Meriwether Lewis, a young Virginian, a friend of the President and his former private secretary. Lewis had chosen as a co-commander of the expedition his friend Captain William Clark, a redheaded Indian fighter, doubtless the most unconventional speller who has ever kept important records. Both Lewis and Clark were experienced frontier campaigners of proven courage, ability, and integrity.

In his message asking Congress to vote funds for this exploration, Jefferson had said that the Indians along the Missouri "furnish great supplies of furs and peltry to the trade of another nation." He instructed Lewis to make treaties with the Indians which would divert that trade to the United States, and made it plain that the commercial possibilities of the country (and that meant beaver) were to be an important part of his investigation.

Adventure of the Two Captains

We have seen how Captain Robert Gray established an American claim to the Columbia in 1792, when he sailed into the estuary and named it after his ship. The British also laid claim to the river, based on the exploration of Alexander Mackenzie, who believed it was the Columbia that he had quit to begin the long portage that led him to Dean Channel in 1793. An additional British claim was based on Vancouver's exploration. He had sent one of his lieutenants into the estuary, but had judged it to be an arm of the sea. Jefferson hoped to settle these conflicting claims through the Lewis and Clark Expedition.

About fifty men were in the American party, most of them chosen from frontier garrisons of the army by reason of their experience as woodsmen. They were a hardy lot. During the twenty-eight months they were to spend navigating wild and unknown rivers, among forbidding mountains, and exposed to constant danger, only one man was lost and he died of a "biliose corlick" shortly after the start. The flotilla consisted of two large board canoes, called pirogues, and a fifty-foot keelboat. There was a plentiful supply of presents for gaining the Indians' goodwill toward their Great White Father. Red military jackets and medals bearing the President's likeness proved to be especially powerful lures for chiefs. Wonder of wonders among the armament was a rapid-fire air gun that never failed to astound the natives. Lewis' Newfoundland dog, Scammon, was another source of wonder. He was the biggest dog any Indian had ever seen.

The lower reaches of the Missouri were familiar to such fur dealers as Manuel Lisa, the Chouteaus, and others who traded with tribes along the river and those living inland within easy reach of St. Louis. But the upper river, beyond the villages of the Mandan and Hidatsa Indians, was unknown except for a few bits of information gleaned from far-ranging Hudson's Bay and North West Company trappers, who were more interested in concealing the sources of their rich hauls of beaver than in making them known to rivals. Charts made by Vancouver, of which the expedition had copies, furnished sketchy knowledge of the mouth of the Columbia, but the river was completely uncharted between the Mandan towns and the Pacific Coast.

All through the summer the Lewis and Clark party made its laborious way up the Missouri. When fall came on, with foliage beginning to show gay colors and great flocks of wildfowl flying southward, they went ashore for the winter and built Fort Mandan, near the lower of the two Mandan towns. A short distance upriver were several villages of Hidatsas, a tribe designated in the sign language of the Plains Indians by an open hand held over the abdomen, a gesture the French translated as "Gros Ventres"—in English, "big bellies." These people, as well as the Mandans, lived permanently in large, round huts made of logs plastered with clay. The horses were stabled inside at night to prevent their being stolen. Since the walls were without windows, these homes, though warm and snug, were highly odorous.

The men's quarters at Fort Mandan were made comfortable by huge log fires, and the Americans spent a very pleasant winter, in spite of the bitterly cold weather. They were astonished to see the Indians going about clothed in only buffalo robe and G-string. Game was so abundant that there was never a scarcity of meat. The Indian neighbors were friendly and spent many leisurely hours about the fort. This was especially true of the Mandan girls, who boasted fairer skins than the usual run of squaws. They proved to possess irresistible charms for this group of vigorous young men with few exacting duties, and the party came through the winter in excellent health and spirits.

A French Canadian, Cruzatte, was a fiddler and furnished music of a sort for frequent dances, and York, Clark's huge Negro slave, amused audiences throughout the long winter with his vaudeville act in which he danced hoedowns or played the part of a malevolent demon. York was an especial favorite with the ladies.

In the course of the winter, the party was enlarged by the hiring of Toussaint Charbonneau as interpreter. He had lived for years among the Hidatsas as a trader, and had two Indian wives.

One of them was a young squaw named Sacajawea, who had been captured as a young girl from the Shoshoni branch of the Snake tribe. She has become a legend in western history because of her great contribution to the later success of the expedition as guide and interpreter. During the winter at Fort Mandan, Sacajawea gave birth to a son, assisted in her ordeal by a dose of powdered snake rattles prescribed by Captain Lewis. The baby was named Pompey and continued with the party to the end. He became a great pet, especially of Clark, who took him to St. Louis on the return and sent him to school.

The Americans bade farewell to their Indian friends and went on up the Missouri in the early spring of 1805. There were now thirty-one men, plus Sacajawea and her baby. The rest had been sent to St. Louis with boats loaded with reports, natural history specimens, and beaver pelts. The first major obstacle to be met upriver was the Great Falls of the Missouri. More than a month was required to carry the boats and baggage around this eighteen-mile cataract. Shortly after passing the falls, the explorers reached Three Forks, where the Jefferson, Madison, and Gallatin Rivers meet to form the Missouri. Here Clark noted "emence numbers of beaver."

Following the westernmost of the three rivers, which they named after the President, the captains were at length convinced that waters flowing to the Pacific could not be reached without making a long carry. For this, they must have horses. Sacajawea told them that the horses could be bought from her tribe, whose country they had now entered. After considerable search, Lewis, scouting ahead, overtook a band of these elusive people and persuaded them to go back with him to join his companions. As soon as Sacajawea saw the visitors, she recognized them as the same band from which she had been captured as a young girl. Its chief was her own brother. Lewis' journal says that she ran to him and wept as she embraced him. This happy reunion calmed the fears of the Snakes, who had taken the Americans for an invading war party.

Guided by Sacajawea's people and with the help of their horses, the party threaded its way through a maze of rugged mountains, finally coming down to a small stream in which they found a stranded salmon. This was a fish that had come up from the Pacific and was at the end of its long spawning run. The explorers had crossed the Continental Divide and at long last were on the Pacific watershed. The small stream led them to the Salmon River, which runs to the Snake. After a rough run down the Snake in newly made dugouts, they floated out at last on the broad expanse of the Columbia River.

The run from here down to the sea was no holiday excursion, but their best watermen were by now experts at running dangerous rapids, and they won safely through miles of extremely rough water to where the river grew calmer. On the seventh of November, 1805, Clark, sitting as always with his notebook on his knee, made a jubilant entry: "Ocian in view! Oh, the joy!"

The great adventure had blazed a trail across the continent; it had established for the United States a firm claim to the great unmapped country west of the Rockies, and to the legendary river which Captain Gray had discovered—the outlet to the Orient for the treasure yet to be garnered. For treasure there was in plenty. Lewis, in his report to the President on returning later to St. Louis, would write that the country he had explored "is richer in beaver and otter than any country on earth." Pelts from all this region could be shipped by way of the Columbia to reach Canton, the great Chinese fur market, months ahead of shipments starting at the same time from Montreal.

The explorers spent an extremely wet winter in a log shelter which they named Fort Clatsop. Their Indian neighbors were unattractive people, sullen, crawling with vermin, infected with disease, and habitual thieves. They had to be borne with as good grace as possible, however, for they were too numerous to risk offending, and might prove useful in emergencies, as they were extremely skillful at navigating their big wooden canoes through seemingly impassable water. On only one occasion did Lewis lose patience with them. He discovered a pair making off with his dog, Scammon. This was too much to be borne. Flying into a rage, he sent three men after the thieves, with orders to shoot if they did not release the pet at once. When the Indians saw that Lewis was serious, they fled into the woods, and Scammon ran joyfully back to his master.

There was plentiful evidence that the occupants of Fort Clatsop were not the first white men to visit these parts. The local inhabitants had metal cooking pots, knives, and other manufactured articles, and some of them wore bits of cast-off sailors' clothing. One young squaw proudly exhibited a tattoo on her arm reading, "J. BOWMAN."

At the end of March, Fort Clatsop was abandoned and the party set out on the homeward journey in two big Indian canoes and their own dugouts. May and June were spent with the Nez Percés ("pierced noses"), a superior tribe with whom they had left horses and trade goods on the westward march. These good Indians had taken excellent care of the property left in their care, and it was very welcome, for the expedition was all but bare of means to pay their way home.

Now they went on their way with sixty-five good horses, plenty of trade goods, and two Nez Percé guides. A week's travel brought them to a campsite of the previous year that they had named Travelers' Rest. Here they divided into two detachments which went by different routes to an appointed meeting at the junction of the Missouri and the Yellowstone. Clark explored the Yellowstone with part of his men. His other people recovered canoes they had hidden a year ago and went down the Missouri. On the way, they joined Lewis' party, which they met at Great Falls. Lewis himself had parted from them to explore a river that flowed into the Missouri from the north.

On the outbound journey, he had judged that this river might be the means of cutting in ahead of Canadian trappers to stop their progress westward. He had named it Maria's (or Marias) River as a compliment to Miss Maria Wood, a sweetheart left behind in Virginia. In his journal, Lewis offered her an apology, expressing the opinion that the Marias was unworthy of such a charming sponsor. "It is true," he wrote, "that the hue of the waters of this turbulent stream but illy comport with the pure, celestial virtues and amiable qualifications of that lovely fair one." It is not recorded whether Miss Wood received the compliment with pride or with mirth.

With Lewis on this detour to the Marias were three men, George Drouillard and two brothers named Fields. They had a rough time. The Marias proved to be too short and rocky to be used as a means of cutting off the westward progress of Canadian trappers. Lewis had hoped to find it an important river that came from far in the north. But he found plenty of beavers along its course, and in later years it yielded many "plews," or pelts.

On the way down the Marias to rejoin their main party, Lewis and his three companions ran into a band of eight Blackfeet, who told them in sign talk that a large band of their tribe was nearby. The Indians seemed to be friendly, and they all camped together that night.

In the early morning hours Joseph Fields, who was on watch, carelessly laid his rifle down, and an Indian seized it and ran into the woods. At the same moment the weapons of the three other Americans were snatched from beside them as they slept. Reuben Fields, waking instantly, overtook the man who had stolen his brother's rifle, wrenched it out of his hands and sank a knife into his body. Fortunately the other three weapons were soon recovered, and Lewis brought down one of the fleeing Blackfeet with a quick shot. These were the only fatalities inflicted on Indians in the whole course of the expedition.

The Blackfeet had abandoned all their arms and equipment, and it was immediately piled on the fire and burned. Selecting four of the best of the Indians' horses and stampeding the others, the Americans mounted and rode hard that day and until two o'clock the next morning. After a short rest, they pressed on at daylight, still expecting to be attacked.

As they neared the Missouri they heard rifle shots, which they were relieved to find came from a hunting party of their own people, and together they went down the river. When they joined Clark at the Yellowstone, the now united expedition went on without further incident to St. Louis, where on September 23,

1806, Clark recorded in his journal that they received a "harty welcom."

The expedition had achieved all that President Jefferson had hoped for. As a reward, he appointed Lewis governor of Upper Louisiana with headquarters at St. Louis, and Clark was named superintendent of Indian affairs for that territory.

In the fall of 1809, Lewis started for Washington to confer with the Secretary of War. On the journey, he put up for the night at a backwoods inn on the Natchez Trace, a rough road infested with highwaymen that led to Nashville, Tennessee. In the early morning hours he was found dying in his bedroom with two pistol wounds in his body. Some evidence indicated suicide, some, murder. The circumstances of his tragic death have remained a mystery to this day.

With the exception of a term as governor of Missouri, Clark served as superintendent of Indian affairs in St. Louis until his death. He was always a staunch friend of the western tribes, and "the redheaded chief" became a legend among them. Indians coming to St. Louis never failed to seek him out, and his door was always open to them.

Colter's Hell

As the Lewis and Clark adventurers were about to start from the mouth of the Yellowstone on the last lap of their journey home, a dugout came upriver around a bend and put in to shore. It was manned by two Americans who were on their way to trap beaver in the Rockies. They said they would like to take on as a third partner someone who was familiar with the country where they planned to operate.

John Colter, one of the expedition's best men, had come to love the roving life he had led for the past two years and was more than willing to join them. With the consent of the captains, he went back up the river with the two trappers, and the three spent the fall and winter on the Yellowstone, where they made a fine haul of pelts. When spring came Colter decided he had had enough, and started alone down the Missouri headed for St. Louis. At the mouth of the Platte, he met a brigade commanded by Manuel Lisa, one of the shrewdest and most successful of the St. Louis fur traders. Fired by the glowing reports of Lewis and Clark about trapping possibilities on the upper Missouri, Lisa had organized this brigade to try out the new territory.

The lure of the mountains had got into Colter's blood. Like an old sailor unable to resist the urge to go back to sea, he joined Lisa and once again turned toward the Rockies. The brigade went up the Yellowstone to the mouth of the Bighorn, where they built Fort Manuel, the first permanent American post of the mountain fur trade. They found plenty of beaver.

Late in November, after the freezing of the streams made trapping impossible, Lisa sent Colter out alone to interest local Indians in doing some spring trapping for Fort Manuel. The exact route he followed in his adventurous wanderings is uncertain, for he left no written record and told his story differently at various times. He seems to have been a confirmed romancer. It is certain that he went up the Bighorn to the Stinking Water, a river now known by the less forthright name of Shoshone. At its source near the present eastern boundary of Yellowstone Park, he passed through a region dotted with mineral springs and geysers now called Colter's Hell, and went on through country that has become a part of the park. After his return to Fort Manuel, the stories he told of the wonders he had seen gained him a reputation as a tremendous liar.

In the summer after his return, Colter went out again to encourage trade in the vicinity of the Three Forks. Here he made friends with some Crow Indians, and started with a band of them to trade their furs at Fort Manuel. On the way they were attacked by a large war party of Blackfeet. The battle was going badly for the Crows until they were reinforced by a strong band of their tribe, who turned the tide. Colter took a prominent part in the fight and accounted for his full share of the enemy, who retreated after suffering severe casualties. His part in this battle had much to do with turning the Blackfeet into bitter enemies of the whites, an enmity that made them the scourge of American trappers for years to come.

Colter grew to hate the tribe, and in the year following his first brush with them is said to have sent many a Blackfoot warrior down the sunset trail. The Blackfeet returned his hatred whole-heartedly. Who can blame them? From the Indians' point of view, these invaders from another world, with their superior knowledge and weapons, were taking possession of the country that had always been their own hunting grounds. The Indian's immemorial way of life was being changed against his will, and naturally he resisted. To be sure, his methods of resistance were cruel and barbarous, but these were the only methods he knew and the same methods he used in fighting other Indians.

One day when Colter and a partner named Potts were cruising a stream near Three Forks, a large party of Blackfeet appeared on the bank and ordered them ashore. Colter, seeing no chance of escape, paddled his canoe to the bank; but Potts refused to come in, shot one of the Indians from his canoe, and was immediately riddled with arrows. The Blackfoot chief, bored by this unimaginative murder and recognizing in the captive a particular foe, decided that Colter should provide a bit of entertainment before he died. He was stripped naked, given a head start, and ordered to run for his life.

As he told the story afterward, he ran for six miles through bushes and thorny cactus, followed by the yelling Indians. One by one the exhausted warriors dropped behind until only a single pursuer remained in the race. Suddenly Colter wheeled and seized the man's spear. In the struggle that followed, the shaft of the weapon was broken. Colter succeeded in wrenching the blade end from the Indian's grasp and plunged it into his body. Leaving his enemy writhing on the ground, he ran on, with the other Indians far to the rear. When he reached the Madison River, he dived in and came up under a raft of floating driftwood. He was able to breathe by sticking his nose into a narrow space between two logs, so he lay there all day, while the frustrated Indians beat the bushes up and down the stream and even walked across the logs under which he was hiding. In all probability, Colter's life-saving shelter was a broken-off section of beaver dam.

When night came on, the Blackfeet gave up the search, and

Colter silently swam far downstream, climbed out onto the bank, and struck out overland for Fort Manuel, some two hundred miles away. He traveled all that night and for seven days more, naked, barefoot, and unarmed, his feet lacerated by sharp stones and pierced by cactus thorns, keeping life in his body by eating berries and roots. Over the last few hundred yards he was carried by his amazed companions, who had run out of the fort to help him.

Here we have perhaps the first of the many tall tales for which the mountain men became famous. Colter's story is certainly founded on fact, but how much his fancy added to it is anyone's guess. His description of the things he saw in the Yellowstone Park region is the first account of the natural wonders that have since fascinated millions of tourists. In some versions of his story, his hiding place becomes a beaver lodge instead of a raft of driftwood. It is doubtful that a grown man could squeeze through an escape tunnel to get into the interior of a lodge.

John Colter's adventurous selling campaign among the Indians around Fort Manuel paid off handsomely for a time. The streams were rich in beaver, and the fort's own trappers, together with Colter's Crow friends, brought in a wealth of pelts, which Lisa took down to St. Louis at the end of the season. His success attracted new capital, thus enabling him to form the St. Louis Missouri Fur Company.

The new firm sent its first brigade up the river in the summer of 1809. There were some three hundred in the party, the largest yet to go to the mountains. The men were furnished outfit and transportation by the company, and were to trap in small, independent groups, one quarter of their take to be divided among themselves.

Fort Manuel was their main base, and a small post was built at Three Forks. All around both posts lay virgin beaver country. Everything seemed to promise a successful operation—everything except the Blackfeet. Time and again these bloodthirsty warriors wiped out small parties trapping the nearby streams. At the Three Forks post, a party of eighteen was attacked, and five of the men with all their furs were lost. George Drewyer, who had come safely through the perils of the Lewis and Clark Expedition, was killed, along with two others of the small party he was leading. At Three Forks the men hardly dared go beyond sight of the stockade, and the post was finally abandoned.

The survivors went across the Continental Divide to the Snake River. Beavers were plentiful here, but after the coming of winter put an end to trapping they found game so scarce that they were reduced to eating horsemeat. Many deserted, preferring the risk of falling into the hands of the Indians to remaining in such dangerous country. In the spring of 1811, the remnant gave up and started for St. Louis, which only a few of them managed to reach. The post on the Bighorn was also abandoned because of the enmity of the Blackfeet, and for a time the whole of the rich beaver country beyond the Mandan towns was closed to trappers by the tribe that John Colter had first antagonized.

Astoria

From the first years of bartering for pelts along the lower St. Lawrence, beaver-trapping had moved steadily westward. As one hunting ground was trapped out, the hunters moved on to a new one. The movement was slow but constant, and always toward the Pacific. By the time of the return of Lewis and Clark, which marks the beginning of the great period of American fur trade, profitable trapping areas had been pushed westward to the Rockies.

Now the valleys of that rugged mountain chain were being invaded by fur hunters—Hudson's Bay men in the north, Nor'westers in the middle ranges, and Americans to the south. These American trappers were the vanguard that led the march of the new republic acrosss the western plains, over the Rocky Mountains, and to the Pacific Ocean. And the lure that led them westward was not gold, or timber, or land, but always the soft, rich fur of the beaver.

Wherever the hunting grounds of the rival groups overlapped,

Fort Laramie, built on a fork on the North Platte, was a permanent trading post and became an outpost on emigrant trails.

unrestrained competition plus the often violent enmity of local tribes made the scramble for beaver pelts a highly uncertain and dangerous business. Now there came into the field a commercial genius who proposed to bring order out of the prevailing chaos by gaining control of the entire fur trade. He would build a chain of posts, under one management, reaching from the Rockies to the mouth of the Columbia.

John Jacob Astor, a young German immigrant, had landed at Baltimore in the spring of 1784 to seek his fortune. He brought with him a small stock of musical instruments, and traded them for beaver pelts which he sold at a handsome profit in London. In a few years he built this small beginning into a fortune. Through his association with the fur interests of Montreal, he was able to avoid the high British tariff against American furs by making his shipments from Canada. By 1800 he had become a power in this trade. In 1810 he founded the Pacific Fur Company, with the object of dominating the entire industry.

As a first step, Astor planned to gain control of trapping in the Columbia watershed, and to use the river as an outlet for shipments to China. Alexander Mackenzie's crossing of the continent in 1793, as well as Vancouver's explorations on the Pacific Coast, had established a British claim to the country that Astor meant to take over. All the Northwest beyond the Rockies was loosely called Oregon. Its boundaries were completely unfixed, but the British held that it included the Columbia River.

Astor proposed to accomplish his control of the Columbia by launching two well-financed expeditions, one to go overland from St. Louis to the river's mouth, the other to go there by sea around Cape Horn. His seaborne expedition, completely equipped for trading, sailed from New York on the *Tonquin* in September, 1810, reached the Columbia after a stormy seven-month voyage, and built Fort Astoria on the southern bank of the estuary.

Astor's overland party, some sixty strong, left St. Louis in March, 1811, and paddled and pushed its way up the Missouri as far as Grand River, in present-day South Dakota. There they struck overland to the southwest in order to avoid the dreaded Blackfeet in the vicinity of Three Forks.

After a long and difficult march to the Snake River, the party again took to the water in dugouts bought from the Indians. Almost at once they got into serious trouble. In the wild canyons of the Snake, the canoes were badly smashed and a great part of the baggage was lost. The disheartened travelers, famished and frozen, broke up into small groups and struggled on westward. More than nine harrowing months after the start, the first group reached Astoria, to be followed at intervals by remnants of their companions. The last seven men reached the post more than a year after the first arrivals.

They found Fort Astoria no happy haven. The first of its long series of disasters had occurred. Shortly after putting ashore the seaborne party at the Astoria site, the *Tonquin* had cruised north to trade with Indians along the coast. Her martinet captain, enraged by the surliness of a band of Chinook Indians, was so rash as to insult them by slapping the chief's face. The next day the

Chinooks returned to the ship in force and began trading their pelts for hunting knives. Nursing their grievances quietly, at an agreed signal they drew the new weapons from under their robes, fell upon the astonished crew, and massacred them all. The fatally wounded ship's clerk crawled to the powder magazine, touched it off, and blew up the ship, together with himself and all the jubilant Indians crowding her decks.

When news of this disaster at length made its way down the coast, the Astorians realized that they were marooned on a far shore without any means of communication or supply. A party of six at once headed for St. Louis to bring news of their predicament to Astor's agents. As they approached the Rocky Mountains on their journey, Indians told them of an easy way over the Wind River Range, a route which proved to be so low and unobstructed that it could be traveled by wagons. This break in the mountains later became famous as South Pass, the gate through which the flood tide of the great American migration flowed westward.

Beyond South Pass the Astorians struck the headwaters of the Platte and followed that river to the Missouri and on to St. Louis, where they arrived ten months after their start. The route that was followed for the first time on this march became the famous Oregon Trail, over which thousands of westering Americans were to travel to reach the rich farming lands of Oregon and the goldfields of California.

Back at the wooden fort on the Pacific Coast, the arrival of the *Beaver*, a second ship sent out by Astor, put the post in business again. Now supplied with the means for trading, brigades went up the Columbia, Willamette, and Spokane, and east as far as the Snake and Clearwater. They made tremendous hauls of beaver.

When news of the *Tonquin*'s loss reached Astor in New York, he made strenuous efforts to continue the support of his far-distant trading post, but could do little. War had broken out between England and the United States, the War of 1812, and the British navy was on watch in Hawaii. With North West Company posts competing over much of its territory, the difficulties of Fort Astoria were formidable. The war had made capture by the British the probable fate of any American vessel attempting to reach it with supplies. A ship fitted out by Astor's agents in London was prevented from leaving port by the refusal of her crew to sail her to the relief of enemies of England. To the dismay of Astor's people, it was learned that the North West Company was fitting out a privateer, the *Isaac Todd*, to sail around Cape Horn to seize Astoria as a spoil of war.

Hard luck seemed always to haunt the affairs of the post. Thoroughly discouraged, Duncan McDougall, the post commander, sold Astoria with all its equipment, stores, and outposts to representatives of the North West Company. McDougall, Canadian-born and a former Nor'wester, stayed on as an employee of the new owners.

A month after the sale, Alexander Henry the Younger, of whom we have read earlier, arrived at the post. He had come overland from Fort William, which had replaced Grand Portage as the field headquarters of the North West Company. The last few pages of Henry's journal tell the story of the comic-opera proceedings that now began. He found the Chinook Indians most unpleasant, especially the women, who were filthy, disease-ridden, and completely uninhibited. The Chinooks had acquired a smattering of English. The usual word of greeting was, "Hoahya-clahk," a legacy from Meriwether Lewis, who was accustomed to greet his fellow commander of a morning with, "How are you, Clark?"

Chief Comcomly, "king" of the local band, was "a troublesome beggar," strutting about in his scarlet officer's coat, Chinese hat, and white trousers, selling his daughter's favors to McDougall at a ruinous price.

A year after Henry's arrival, a large ship was sighted standing in over the bar at the mouth of the estuary. This, Henry thought, must be the *Isaac Todd*, sent by his own company to capture the fort from the Americans. Mr. Halsey, a clerk, hurried out in a small boat to tell her captain that he need not unlimber his guns—

the post had already changed ownership. Late that night the watchers ashore heard loud and raucous singing on the water, followed at length by the sound of a boat grating on the shore. Mr. Halsey, himself and his boat's crew feeling mellow from the hospitality tendered them aboard, staggered into the fort to report that their visitor was not the *Todd*, but His Majesty's sloop of war *Raccoon*, Captain Black commanding, come to wrest the stronghold of Astoria from the grasp of the rascally Americans. The captain and his officers were disappointed to learn that the fortress had already passed into British hands, and that they had been cheated out of the fun of a fight.

When Henry rowed out to the ship the next day to meet the captain, he was surprised to find that John McDonald of Garth, a senior North West partner, was aboard, in poor shape as the result of an explosion that had occurred during the voyage. His arms were swathed in bandages, his flaming red locks cut short, and his face blistered and disfigured. In spite of his wounds, Garth came ashore and took command. A few nights later, Captain Black and his principal officers arrived at the fort, in a bad mood and very drunk. Amid blasts of seagoing profanity, they reported that their boat had run afoul of a boulder far down the beach, and they had been obliged to stumble in the dark along a wet tidal flat littered with rocks and driftwood.

The next morning, after the doughty captain had taken a good look at the flimsy wooden stockade, his mood changed to disgust. "Great God Almighty!" he exclaimed. "Is this the fort I've heard so much about? Why, damme, I could knock it down in a couple of hours with a fourpounder!" When his fury had simmered down, he took possession in the name of King George, ran up the Union Jack, broke a bottle of Madeira on the flagpole, and rechristened the post Fort George. Old Chief Comcomly took a dim view of the proceedings, declaring that his son-in-law McDougall was an old woman for having surrendered without a fight.

The *Raccoon* tarried for a month, a visit enlivened by much entertaining between ship and shore. Henry noted of the *Raccoon*'s officers, "Famous fellows for grog, they are!" The ship finally upped anchor and spread her sails. Fort George gave her a farewell seven-gun salute as she bore away, and reverted to monotonous waiting for the *Isaac Todd*.

The post was undersupplied and overmanned, and it was decided to send half the personnel, under command of McDonald of Garth, to Fort William in Canada. The overland brigade pushed off up the Columbia in the early summer of 1814, leaving Alexander Henry in charge at Astoria. He was not too happy over the situation. "Here we are left to the sport of fortune," he writes, "at the mercy of chance, on a barbarous coast, among natives more inclined to murder us for our property than to assist us."

One morning four Indians came in to report that their canoe had passed a ship a few miles up the coast. They could plainly see men walking about her decks, and among them a woman with yellow hair! This Henry dismissed as a bit of Chinook daydreaming. That afternoon the vessel sailed into the river and dropped anchor. Henry, assured by signals that she was a friendly craft, rowed out to her and went aboard. It was the *Isaac Todd* at last! He found the decks deserted, but at length Donald McTavish, a senior North West partner, appeared—and clinging to his arm was a woman with blond hair! The astonished Henry, who had not seen a white woman in years, was forthwith introduced to Miss Jane Barnes, whom McTavish had met casually in a bar in Portsmouth, England.

When the captain of the *Todd* finally came on deck, his greeting was far from cordial. There was bad blood, it seemed, between McTavish and the captain. In fact, there was bad blood between McTavish and everybody else aboard, with the exception of Miss Barnes. When Henry, McTavish, and the lady finally went ashore, the appearance of the first white woman ever to set foot on the banks of the Columbia took the hard-bitten frontiersmen by storm, including the Chinooks. By right of seniority McTavish assumed command, but he continued to occupy his quarters aboard ship, making daily visits to the post accompanied always by Miss Barnes.

Henry's journal reports in detail some interesting events of the next few weeks. Discipline broke down, with much inebriety and quarreling among the employees.

The *Dolly*, the post's jolly boat, was rechristened *Jane*. Chief Comcomly's son became hopelessly infatuated and offered a hundred sea otter skins for Miss Barnes' hand. He promised that she should be mistress over all his other wives, and that he would never make her carry wood, draw water, or dig for roots. She would be allowed to sit at ease from sunup to sundown smoking as many pipes of tobacco as she wished, and would always have fat salmon, elk meat, and anchovies to eat. In spite of these tempting blandishments, Jane spurned him. Then he planned to abduct her, but his plot was discovered and foiled. His father, the chief, demanded of McDougall the final installment of his daughter's purchase price, and milked the canny Scot of fifteen guns, plus "a great deal of other property." In spite of the completion of this sale to the satisfaction of the vendor, the lady was seized by her brothers and carried off to her ancestral wigwam.

Concerning his personal relations with Jane, Henry's diary is silent until we come to this laconic entry: "About sunset, the jolly boat took Mr. McTavish aboard alone; Jane of course remained, having taken up her lodgings in my room." Mr. McTavish took the situation in his stride. His relations with Captain Smith later became so violently strained that quarters for him were prepared at the fort, and shortly after occupying them he consoled himself by forming an alliance with a Chinook widow.

One evening Alexander Henry sat down to write what proved to be the last entry in his journal: "May 21, 1814. Coniah and other Clatsops brought back some stolen things. We clothed the chief, and gave him a writing in lieu of the American one, which I threw into the fire before him. . . . The weather cleared up—" The next day, while sailing to the *Isaac Todd*, the jolly boat was capsized in a sudden gale and Henry, McTavish, and five others were drowned.

The "writing" that Henry burned was a complete roster of the Lewis and Clark party, written by Lewis and left with Chief Coniah shortly before the departure of the Americans from Fort

Clatsop. It would have made a priceless addition to the nation's historic documents.

The treaty that ended the War of 1812 restored Fort Astoria to the Pacific Fur Company, but Astor had by then given up his idea of controlling the western fur trade from the Columbia, and the English continued to operate the post. In 1817 Astor's American Fur Company allied itself with the Chouteaus, masters of the St. Louis trapping interests, and the new alliance extended its business to the Pacific, but it never again occupied the fort at the mouth of the Columbia.

While Astoria failed to realize its founder's ambition to rule the fur trade of the entire West, its establishment tremendously strengthened the United States' claim to the Columbia River country, and was a weighty argument in the negotiations with England that later officially recognized Oregon as a part of the American Union. Again we have an example of the influence of the beaver on the westward expansion of the republic.

March of the Mountain Men

The American beaver trappers who led the way across the "Great American Desert" and through the Rocky Mountains were based mainly at St. Louis, headquarters of the fur companies that employed them or supplied those who were free trappers. The Astorians had gained a precarious lodgment on the western coast, but the tremendous area between the Mississippi and the Pacific was still largely an unexplored wilderness, occupied by a few far-ranging Canadian trappers and many tribes of roving Indians. The penetration of this wilderness by the mountain men marks the great period of the American fur trade, a span of years running from the early nineteenth century to the flood tide of emigration just before the war with Mexico.

The glowing reports brought back by Lewis and Clark about the hundreds of beaver to be found in the headwaters of the Missouri started a procession of trappers up the muddy river, bound for

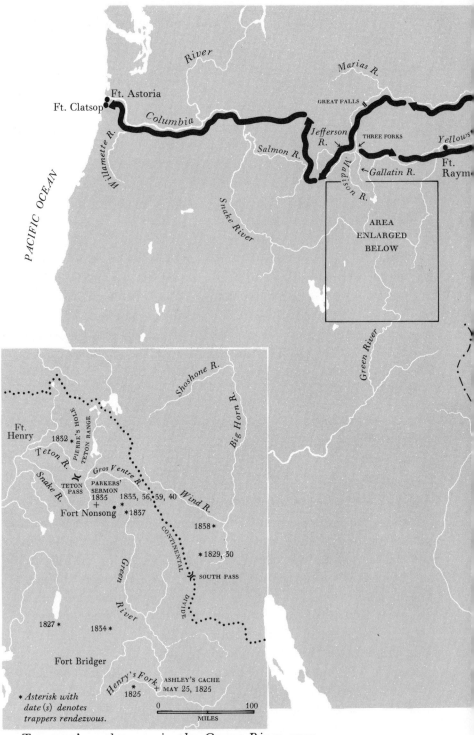

PACIFIC OCEAN

Ft. Clatsop
Ft. Astoria

Willamette R.
Columbia
River
Salmon R.
Snake River

Marias R.
GREAT FALLS
Jefferson R.
THREE FORKS
Madison R.
Gallatin R.
Yellows
Ft. Raym

AREA
ENLARGED
BELOW

Green River

Shoshone R.
Big Horn R.

Ft. Henry
1832 ✱
PIERRE'S HOLE
TETON RANGE
Teton R.
Gros Ventre R.
Snake R.
TETON PASS
PARKERS' SERMON
1835 +
Fort Nonsong ●
1833, 36, 39, 40 ✱
✱1837
Wind R.
1838 ✱
1827 ✱
1834 ✱
Green River
CONTINENTAL DIVIDE
✱ 1829, 30
SOUTH PASS

Fort Bridger

✱ Asterisk with
date(s) denotes
trappers rendezvous.

Henry's Fork
1825 ✱
ASHLEY'S CACHE
+ MAY 25, 1825

0   100
MILES

Trappers' rendezvous in the Green River area.

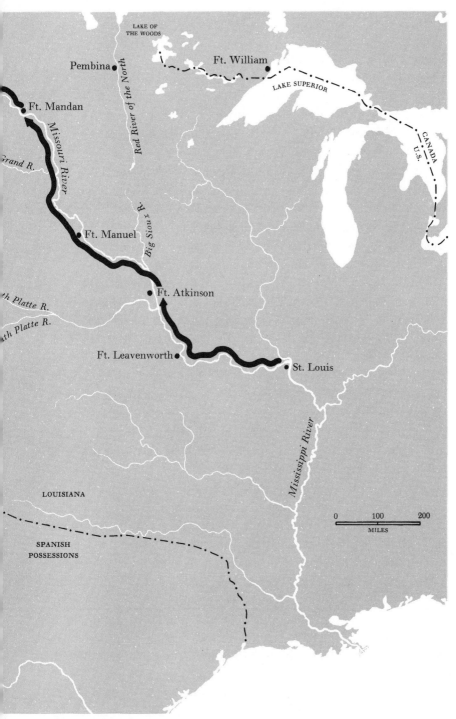

West with the explorers and the mountain men, showing the Lewis and Clark Expedition, 1804–1806.

Great Falls and the country around Three Forks. From there, these men ranged far and wide up the Bighorn and Yellowstone, and into the rugged headwaters of the Snake, Green, and many other rivers. They began the movement that carried a host of Americans into the central Rockies and eventually swept the British from Oregon and the Spaniards from the Southwest.

In the vanguard of this procession was the famous party led by William Ashley and Andrew Henry. Ashley was an influential citizen of St. Louis who, after later making a fortune in the fur trade, retired and represented his district in Congress for many years. Henry was an experienced fur trader who knew something of the country where they proposed to operate.

On February 13, 1822, Ashley published a want ad in a St. Louis newspaper "wishing to enlist one hundred enterprising young men to ascend the River Missouri to its source, there to be employed one, two, or three years." He got the sort of men he wanted—some of the best who ever went up the Missouri after beaver. Many of their names—Jim Bridger, Tom Fitzpatrick, Jedediah Smith, William Sublette—are outstanding in the annals of the American fur trade. A few of them made modest fortunes, some spent the rest of their lives as happy-go-lucky fur trappers, and not a few lost their lives at the hands of the Indians. On the whole, they were a remarkable crew.

The usual practice of St. Louis trading companies was to employ their men at salaries of two to four hundred dollars a year. But Ashley's men were not on salary; they were free trappers, paying half their yearly catch to the company in return for transportation and outfit. It was a safe bet that Ashley and Henry would get a good share of the other half in exchange for clothing, whiskey, and "foofaraw" for the Indian girls.

The party went up the Missouri to the mouth of the Yellowstone in the fall of 1822, built a stockade which they named Fort Henry, and began operations. During the winter, the Blackfeet massacred several small groups trapping on nearby streams, but beavers were as thick as fleas on a dog, and the pelts piled up in the storeroom at Fort Henry.

The following spring, Ashley took a fine cargo of fur to St. Louis, and came back up the river with more men and two keelboats loaded with fresh supplies. When he stopped to trade for horses at an Arikara village at the mouth of Grand River, a storm forced him to tie up there for the night and make camp ashore. Early next morning the Arikaras, having decided to repossess the horses they had just sold, opened fire, and in a few minutes killed fifteen of the men and all the animals they had expected to recover. Ashley dropped back down the river and sent young Jedediah Smith to summon help from Fort Henry, and another messenger downriver to Fort Atkinson, the nearest army post. Both messengers got through. Henry came with the men of his post, and Colonel Leavenworth, commander at Fort Atkinson, brought six companies of infantry from his garrison.

After a bombardment of the Arikara village by the army's small cannon, which did little damage but killed an important chief, the Arikaras decided that odds were too great against them and asked for a parley. The terms granted by Leavenworth were so lenient that Ashley's men were outraged, and their mood was so revengeful that the Indians mistrusted them completely. During the night the entire village silently decamped and disappeared up the river. Nearby there was a post of the Missouri Fur Company. Its "bushway" (mountain talk for *bourgeois*) did not fancy having in his neighborhood a band of Indians panting for revenge, and went with his men to the deserted village and burned it to the ground.

With the Arikaras on the warpath and the always hostile Blackfeet farther up the river, the Missouri was closed to Ashley. He returned to St. Louis after sending his men far overland to the valley of the Bighorn. Colonel Leavenworth took his little army back to Fort Atkinson, and Andrew Henry started back to his post on the Yellowstone with a party of eighty men.

Among them was an old graybeard named Hugh Glass, who went out one day to hunt for meat. As he pushed through a thicket of wild plums, he came face-to-face with a she-grizzly with two cubs. She was on him before he could shoot. Before his hunting partner could come to the rescue she had mangled him so badly that there seemed to be no chance that he could live. The brigade, faced with the near approach of winter, went on, leaving two men to stay with the old man till he died. After watching his suffering for a few days, the pair, judging that he could last only an hour or so, took his equipment, left the half-conscious man a supply of meat, and deserted him. When they overtook Henry's party they reported that he was dead.

Months later, old Hugh Glass walked into Henry's fort on the Yellowstone, as chipper as could be and thirsting for revenge. He had recovered from his "fatal" wounds, kept himself alive on berries and wolf-killed buffalo calves, and had made his way two hundred miles to the fort to settle matters with the men who had left him to his fate.

Only one of the pair was at the post. Glass was for slaughtering him at once, but was dissuaded. After all, they argued, this was a mere boy, a raw tenderfoot, ignorant of the ethics of the mountain man, and a likable youth withal. But Glass was determined to get the other one, who unfortunately was at Fort Atkinson, far down the Missouri. So he joined four men who were bound that way and started out again on his mission. They ran into a band of hostile Indians who killed all of them except the old man, who escaped and pressed on, firm in his determination to settle the score with his enemy.

Nearly a year after his battle with the grizzly, Hugh Glass reached his goal, to find that his quarry was now an enlisted man of the Atkinson garrison. After Colonel Leavenworth had set up a drink and pointed out the disadvantages connected with the murder of a soldier of the United States army, the durable old hunter decided to forgo the pleasure of revenge and contented himself with saying, "Well, I guess the dirty skunk ain't worth shootin' after all."

The men Ashley had sent to the Bighorn valley after the Arikara fight were joined there later by Henry's party, who had come on from their Yellowstone post. Henry himself had gone back to St. Louis. Sickened by the hardship and bloodshed that a cargo of beaver pelts had cost, he quit the partnership, leaving Ashley as sole proprietor. At the Bighorn, the trappers spread out along the river, went through South Pass to Green River, and trapped much of the interior Rocky Mountain country. Jedediah Smith and Jim Bridger, two of the best of Ashley's original "enterprising young men," chanced to find Great Salt Lake on one of their hunting marches. Bridger tasted a mouthful of the water, spat it out, and announced with a wry grin that they had discovered an arm of the Pacific Ocean!

The rich harvest of furs that resulted from all this trapping was taken to St. Louis by Tom Fitzpatrick, now a partner of Ashley. When he arrived, he found that Ashley had decided on a new scheme of operation: he would give up fixed trading posts and substitute a yearly trading fair in the mountains, to be supplied by a summer caravan from St. Louis.

In the spring of 1825, he and Fitzpatrick went out with a well-stocked supply train to Henry's Fork of Green River in southwestern Wyoming, the place that had been appointed for the first rendezvous. This first mountain trading fair proved to be a great success, with a haul of nearly ten thousand pounds of beaver pelts, worth some forty-five thousand dollars in St. Louis. At the rendezvous of the following summer, Ashley sold out to Smith, Jackson, and Sublette, all three members of his original party, and retired a wealthy man.

Following this venture of Ashley's came the most prosperous years of the Rocky Mountain fur trade. Each summer during the next decade, hundreds of roving trappers and Indians met supply caravans from St. Louis at some previously appointed spot to barter their furs, engage in two or three weeks of wild revelry, and go back, usually broke, to the mountain fastnesses.

A number of other fur companies, most of them based on St. Louis, came into the field during these years, and the annual gatherings in the mountains grew larger and gaudier from summer to summer. Each of the larger companies sent out its own supply train, but they all set up their trading tents at the same location.

These men who spent their lives in the mountains were a hardy lot. They trapped in the cold weather of fall or spring, huddled around the fire in crude shelters during winter, and were in constant danger from hostile Indians.

Competition for customers grew more and more furious, whiskey more and more plentiful, and trading practices increasingly lawless. The enterprise—and greed—of the fur hunters did not end until the beaver population had been so reduced that trapping was no longer profitable, but this did not come about before the gates of the West had been opened to the great surge of emigration that followed their tracks.

A Trapper's Year

They were a hardy lot, these men who spent their lives in the mountains, trapping in the cold weather of fall and early spring, huddling around the fire in a crude shelter through the bitterly cold winter, and in constant danger from hostile Indians. They would have burst into guffaws if anyone had suggested that they were leading a march of civilization across a continent. They were out for beaver pelts; that was all. That they learned the geography of the country by heart, knew the layout of the river systems, found the passes through the mountains, and showed the way west to settlers was merely a part of the job.

A mountain man's working year began as he set out at the end of rendezvous around the middle of July, perhaps somewhat shaky as a result of several weeks of strenuous social activity. For a grand fling he had doubtless spent all of last season's haul of "plews" (the mountain way of pronouncing *plus*, the French word for "pelt"). Probably his only useful purchases had been a few articles needed to replenish his outfit. His equipment consisted of saddle and bridle, epishemore (saddle blanket), rifle, powder horn, bullet pouch, hunting knife, six traps, flint and steel, buffalo horn filled with castoreum (beaver bait), hatchet, and "possible sack" containing pipe, tobacco, sewing kit, extra moccasins, and other such small necessities. He may have carried along a touch of luxury in the form of coffee, sugar, and whiskey flask, all of which were soon consumed.

He rode an Indian pony, sleek from feeding on sweet meadow grass, and led a pack horse or mule. He may have been followed by a squaw, gaily bedecked with new foofaraw, who rode another pony or mule. She would come in handy to tend camp, cook, mend clothes, and flesh and stretch the plews. With the possible exception of blankets, this was his complete outfit. Till next summer's rendezvous, he would live mostly on fresh meat without salt, and sleep under the stars when the weather was mild. In the winter months he would allow himself the luxury of a makeshift shelter of logs or a tepee of tanned buffalo hide.

A dozen or so men usually kept together for protection during a season, but broke up by twos or threes for actual trapping. Traps were made by blacksmiths along the lines of the modern steel trap, but were heavier and clumsier.

Having selected a likely site for a trap, such as the spillway of a dam or a path made by beavers leaving or entering the pond, the trapper entered the stream some distance away and waded to the chosen spot, in order to avoid leaving any human scent. The trap

Experienced men acquired great skill in selecting the most likely place to set traps and in arranging their sets so the quarry would not be suspicious.

was usually placed near the bank a few inches underwater and anchored by a chain to a stout stick driven into the bottom of the pond some six feet out from shore. A small tree limb was then stuck into the mud so it would hang directly over the trigger.

Now the trapper took from his bait horn a small quantity of castoreum and smeared it over the limb. This is a secretion from two glands situated in the groin of both male and female beavers. Eastern Indians sometimes mixed a small quantity of dried castoreum with their tobacco for the soothing flavor it gave the smoke, and bits of it were used to scent the garments and sleeping robes of many tribes. Both Indians and whites had great faith in it as a sovereign remedy for earache, hiccups, snakebite, colic, gout, toothache, or almost any other human ailment you could name. Castoreum has a sweet, musky odor that is very attractive to beavers and to many other animals. This was the universal trap bait among mountain men, and many of them made their own brand of "medicine" by adding to castoreum the juice of berries or another flavoring, which they believed made it more tempting.

After the setting was in order, the trapper again waded some distance away from it before going ashore to set traps at other locations. This was chilling work in a cold mountain stream, and rheumatism was the mountain man's occupational disease.

Experienced men acquired great skill in selecting the most likely places to set traps and in arranging their sets so the quarry would not be suspicious. At night when the beaver came out of its lodge to feed, it was attracted by the odor of the bait, swam to investigate it, and stepped on the trigger. This released the trap's jaws, which were forced together by a spring and grasped the animal's leg. The startled beaver's first effort was to get back into deeper water, but it was stopped short by the anchor chain, to which a weight was attached that pulled the victim below the surface, where it soon drowned. In the early morning, the captured animals were collected and skinned, all bits of flesh and sinew carefully scraped off, and the skins stretched on a U-shaped willow frame for curing in the sun. This was squaw's work, if the trapper was so lucky as to own a helpmate.

When winter set in and the streams froze over, trapping was impossible. The various small parties assembled at a chosen camp-site, usually a sheltered valley down out of the high mountains where there were plenty of trees for firewood and forage for the horses. Indian ponies could do well enough on a ration of cotton-wood bark. If there was also a meadow of dry bunchgrass, they came through the winter in fair condition. Horses were not native to the country, but were descendants of animals that had long ago strayed from the camps of Spanish explorers. These strays had multiplied and spread in great herds on the plains.

The winter camp was comparatively luxurious. The trappers who had started out together might be joined by others—there was safety in numbers. The men built log cabins, or lived in tepees. Banked around the outside with snow, and with heavy robes hung over the entrance, the tepee made a comfortable winter home, for it was easy to keep warm and was free of drafts. A man might even allow himself the luxury of a bed, with willow "springs" and buffalo robes for bedclothes. Friendly Indians were welcomed, for their women could be hired to care for the plews, mend or make clothes, or do the cooking.

Squaws were good cooks, and in the winter camp, if game was abundant, living was high. The monotonous fare of the trapping season could be varied with pemmican stew, dried berries, hominy puddings, and other delicacies that Indian cooks knew how to concoct. There was no bread, other than perhaps an occasional flapjack of cornmeal.

Protection of the extra meat supply from wolves and other predators was an ever-present problem. Surplus meat was usually hung in trees, but that did not work with tree-climbing animals. The wolverine especially drew the undying hatred of trappers. They called this clever animal "glutton" or "carcajou," credited it with supernatural powers, and half believed it was part devil and part bear. It made a practice of robbing traplines, and no amount of care could keep hung or buried meat away from its ravenous jaws.

With hunting parties on snowshoes, fresh meat was usually easy to provide in winter camp. The favorite food was buffalo

Mountain man, Jim Bridger, was a past master of the incredible yarn told with a straight face.

steaks or chops. At this time of year, the buffalo were in poor condition, and the meat might be lean and tough. Cows were preferred to bulls, but bulls were better eating than no eating, and sometimes had to be used. An overworked whimsy among wintering trappers was, "A hunk of tough bull meat will bounce like a rubber ball."

If no buffalo were in the vicinity, there might be deer, elk, antelope, or smaller animals that were not especially relished but would keep a man from starving. Beaver meat was not often eaten when other game was to be had. Fresh beaver was available only during trapping season, and other more favored meats were usually plentiful then. There came times, however, when no game could be found, and desperate winterers might be driven to eating boiled moccasins, sleeping robes, or even the skin of their pelts. Beaver skins were a last resort, for they made expensive eating. Indians liked dog meat, and most trappers did not shun it if they were hungry.

Evening, with the men lying at ease around the fire, was a time for shoptalk of the "D'ye remember" variety. This is when the mountain men spun the tall tales—or inspired lies—that have remained a part of our heritage.

Jim Bridger was a past master of the incredible yarn told with a straight face. He was one of the first men to travel through the country that is now Yellowstone Park, and the geysers, hot springs, and boiling mud baths he saw there lost nothing in his description of them. In his opinion, "That country is too near hell to be comfortable." Asked how long he had lived in the mountains, Bridger would say : "See that thar hill? When I first came to these parts, it was a deep hole in the ground." Whether he expected anybody to believe his stories made no difference; he loved to tell them and his pals loved to hear them, if only as an excuse for a laugh.

The famous yarn about the petrified forest, probably first spun by Joe Meek, has been credited to perhaps a dozen other mountain Munchausens. Joe told of coming upon a forest in the mountains where everything had turned to stone. Before his astonished eyes stood hundreds of "putrefied" trees in which flocks of "putrefied" birds were singing "putrefied" songs.

Another creative masterpiece described the unsuccessful stalking of a big bull elk. After painfully crawling half a mile to get within range, the hunter took careful aim and fired. The elk went on feeding, completely undisturbed by the shot. Several successive shots were likewise without effect. Convinced that his eyesight was failing, the man got up and walked toward the animal—and bumped squarely against the side of a mountain of clear crystal that stood between him and his quarry. At his feet lay his flattened bullets.

There was a place where any loud noise echoed from a cliff that was so far away it took eight hours for the echo to get back to its starting point. This natural phenomenon made a useful alarm clock. When you went to bed, you could shout, "Time to get up!" and the echo would waken you at sunup.

Jim Beckwourth, a mulatto slave who had broken his bonds and gone west as a young man, lived for years among the Crow Indians and became one of their war chiefs. He was outstanding among his fellow trappers as a braggart and romancer, with himself always in the role of hero. His vivid imagination often triumphed over his veracity, so the fantastic stories he told of his adventures must be taken with reservation.

Jim entertained a deep emotional attachment for a handsome Amazon of his Crow village named Pine Leaf, but she would have none of him. She promised to marry him, however, if he would wait for the fulfillment of a vow that she had made to the Great Spirit. When she was a young girl, her brother had fallen in a battle with the Cheyennes, and she had vowed to remain unmarried until she had avenged his death by taking the scalps of a hundred of his enemies. Pine Leaf rode beside Jim on many war forays, and to help boost her score he often chivalrously permitted her to take scalps that rightly belonged to himself. When she had finally made her quota, she consented to take her place as the favorite among his many wives.

Jim told such outrageous lies that he became notorious even among so many men who were talented in that line. For example, take this one: The mourning of the Crow squaws for relatives lost in a battle with the Cheyennes lasted so long that it got on his nerves. The women slashed their skin, covered their faces with white ashes, and made day and night hideous with their howling. Jim finally could bear the interminable wailing no longer. One night he crept into a Cheyenne village alone and collected the scalps of four sleeping warriors one after another without wakening any other sleepers. Then he yelled the Crow war cry, waved his scalps in the air, and escaped as the confused Cheyennes boiled out of their lodges. His triumphant return with the trophies that avenged the fallen Crow warriors put an end to the grief of the mourners, and allowed them to wash the ashes from their faces.

In later life, Beckwourth settled down in California and dictated his memoirs to a ghost writer. When some of his old cronies in the California mountains heard that Jim had written a book, they took up a collection and sent a man to Sacramento to buy a copy. An unscrupulous clerk, not having the volume in stock, sold the illiterate messenger a Bible. When he returned, Jim's friends assembled to hear the only literate member of the group read their old buddy's story aloud. Opening the Bible at random, he chanced to begin at the fifteenth chapter of Judges, which tells how Samson destroyed the crops of the Philistines by sending into their corn-fields three hundred foxes with firebrands tied to their tails. At this point one of the audience interrupted the reading. "Stop right thar!" he cried. "I'd know that for one of Jim Beckwourth's damned lies anywhere."

Then there were reminiscences, stark or amusing, of things that had happened. The one about Mike Fink is an example. Mike was a quarrelsome bully who had only one close friend, a fellow named Carpenter. They were both crack shots and loved to show off their skill. In a favorite stunt, Mike would stand with a cup of whiskey on top of his head while Carpenter, at seventy paces, shot it off. Then Fink, at the same distance, would shoot a cup off Carpenter's head. They were boon companions until, trapping on the Musselshell River one time, they fell out over mutual admiration for the same squaw. The boys got them to patch up their quarrel, and to show that complete friendship and trust prevailed, Mike proposed that they do their whiskey-shooting stunt. Carpenter agreed, and they drew lots to see who should have the first shot. Mike won, stepped off the seventy paces, took careful aim, and shot Carpenter between the eyes. Fink claimed it was an accident, that faulty loading had caused his poor shooting. But later, he bragged that he had aimed right where his bullet hit. Whereupon a man named Talbot, a friend of Carpenter, shot Fink through the heart.

On the lighter side, there was the time that Joe Meek, shooting from shore, killed a she-grizzly that was feeding on an island in the Siskadee. Joe and his partner stripped off their clothes and swam out to the island to get the hide and some meat. But the grizzly was only wounded, and she chased the two naked men into the river and swam furiously after them. They beat her to shore and took off through the woods with the bear right behind them, all to the hearty amusement of their pals, who were stand-ing on the bank. How the chase ended was of no interest. The point was that the picture of two stark-naked men being chased by an irate grizzly was a sidesplitter.

Late in March, when winter broke, it was time to abandon the comfortable camp and start traveling. The ice that had held the streams in thrall was going out. The soft, thick beaver fur that had developed during the winter was now at its prime, and the beavers were coming out of their lodges to repair dams and to feed on the juicy bark and water-growing plants of spring.

Indians too were hearing the call of the season, and their hunting parties would be roaming the mountains. If hostile, they must be avoided—or fought. Trappers developed great skill in reading sign, in determining from any human tracks they came across what tribe had made them, how many were in the party, whether they were hunting or on the warpath, whether friendly or hostile, and how recently they had passed this way. Was a buffalo herd moving at unusual speed? Were the ears of a deer set at listening position? Were magpies making too much noise to be at ease? Any of these signs might indicate the presence of danger.

The trapper also had to make a mental map of the country through which he was traveling, the relative position of ridges and streams and their relation to rivers. For he must keep moving to find untrapped water, and be able to find his way back to camp or to rendezvous when the time came. Two men could trap out a small stream in a few days and then must find another. They slept where night overtook them.

Osborne Russell, in his book *Journal of a Trapper*, tells of camping one night in a heavy rain. He and his partner, Allen, killed a buffalo bull for supper and tried to roast some of the tough meat over a miserable fire of "a few bits of sage and weeds. . . . We could not find a stick for fuel bigger than a man's thumb." They cooked the meat until it was barely warmed through, and Allen, who always looked on the bright side, observed as he chewed, "Bull meat is dry eating when cooked too much." They used the fresh hide for a bed. This is Russell's description of their night's rest:

> *We spread the bull skin down in the mud in the dryest place we could find and laid down upon it. Our fire was*

immediately put out by the rain and all was Egyptian darkness. We lay tolerably comfortable whilst the skin retained its animal warmth and remained above the surface, but the mud being soft, the weight of our bodies sank it by degrees below the water level, which ran under us on the skin. But we concluded it was best to lie still and keep the water warm that was about us, for if we stirred, we let in the cold water, and if we removed our bed, we were more likely to find a worse instead of a better place, as it rained very hard all night.

A buffalo hide fresh from the warm carcass made a good bed if you wrapped it tightly around you. Elk hide was not so good for this purpose. If it got wet, it shrank until it was close to your body and then became so hard that it was difficult to get out of bed next morning. Bearskins made good bedcovers. Grizzlies were abundant in the mountains, especially where there were clumps of wild plum or cherry trees. Russell writes of having frequently seen as many as seven or eight feeding in one grove in the early morning. You never knew whether they would go on feeding calmly or attack you. They were fierce, powerful brutes and it might take several bullets to stop one unless you knew just where to aim.

The spring hunt continued until summer came to the mountains, when snow melted on the slopes, ran down the valleys, and turned the streams into raging torrents. The fur of the beavers was no longer prime. The hair had grown thin and short and was not acceptable to traders. The time had come to quit the high places and go down into some warm, lush valley that had been chosen as the location for the summer trading fair. If he had collected a good haul of prime pelts and been lucky enough to escape being robbed of them, together with his scalp, by hostile Indians, the trapper set out for the rendezvous with his pack horse loaded and his heart light. Even if he had lost the spoils of his season's hunting to the Blackfeet, he knew he could have his fling and replenish his outfit on the promise of next season's trapping. Rendezvous time was the grand payoff for the hardships he had endured during the year.

Rendezvous

Pierre's Hole is a beautiful valley on the eastern border of Idaho, watered by numerous tree-lined creeks that flow into Henry's Fork of the Snake River (not to be confused with Henry's Fork of the Green). On the valley's eastern edge, the lordly Teton Range towers fourteen thousand feet into the sky to present one of the supreme spectacles of the Rocky Mountains. In this lovely valley was held the rendezvous of 1832. Though it was perhaps especially marked by dramatic events, it may be taken as an example of these annual gatherings during the high years of the Rocky Mountain fur trade.

Along the river stood the company trading stores, yet to be supplied with the goods that their caravans were bringing from St. Louis. Here were partners and employees of the Rocky Mountain Fur Company, the American Fur Company, and other smaller outfits. Hundreds of company men and free trappers had come in from the far reaches of the mountains to barter the spoils of their season's hunting for a few necessities and a big spree. Here also were Indians of many friendly tribes: Flatheads, Crows, Bannocks, Nez Percés, Snakes. Each tribe had put on a colorful show as it came in sight of the encampment, with chiefs in full war panoply, painted warriors prancing on their gaily decorated ponies, the women in freshly whitened and decorated doeskins, dogs barking excitedly, and old squaws screeching encouragement to the horse herds. After curvetting around the field, they had set up their tepees and settled down to waiting for the show to begin.

But a cloud of gloom hung over the camp: there was no firewater. There would be a copious supply in the caravans of both major fur companies, but they were long overdue. Whichever caravan arrived first with liquor would get the cream of the trade.

To relieve his own and his partners' anxiety, Tom Fitzpatrick rode off alone to find the Rocky Mountain Company's caravan, tell Bill Sublette, its commander, of the situation, and urge him to hurry. Fitzpatrick found Sublette on Laramie Fork of the Platte, four hundred miles east of the rendezvous. After telling him of the necessity for speed, he started back to Pierre's Hole to assure his people that their supplies would be in shortly.

On the morning of July 8, Sublette's caravan swept into Pierre's Hole in a cloud of dust, to the accompaniment of yelling men, guns shooting at the sky, jingling harness, and braying mules. The supplies of the Rocky Mountain Company were in ahead of any others, and it would reap the richest harvest.

This joyous welcome was somewhat dampened when it was realized that Fitzpatrick was not at the camp, where Sublette had expected to find him, nor was he with Sublette's caravan, where his partners thought he would be. "Fitz" was a supremely skillful master of mountain craft, but the country was full of Blackfeet, and it was feared that the old master had at last lost his scalp. That same afternoon, however, the missing man stumbled into camp, "his body so thin," said one of his friends, "you could count the knobs on his backbone from the front."

When Fitz had left Sublette at the Sweetwater, he was riding a good horse and leading another. Soon after fording Green River, he had run into a village of Gros Ventres, close relatives of the Blackfeet and, like them, always hostile. Fitz had escaped their attack by pushing his horses until they could go no farther. Abandoning the exhausted animals, he hid in a crevice in the rocks as his pursuers scoured the forest around him, many times coming within a few steps of his hiding place. At night he started on, but again ran afoul of the camp of the Gros Ventres. He went back to his crack in the rocks, lay there all day, and at night got clean away. After crossing miles of tortuous country cut by gulches and ravines, he came to the Snake. Here he made a raft in order to cross without wetting his powder, but the swift current tore apart the fragile craft and he lost his rifle, shot pouch, and tinderbox.

Finally gaining the other side by swimming, he went on, keeping himself alive by eating buds and roots. One day he found the remains of a buffalo that wolves had left. Having no means of making a fire, he ate the carrion raw. His moccasins wore out, and he wrapped his feet in strips of felt cut from his hat. Through all this he was never lost, and finally made his way, more dead than alive, to his friends.

The rendezvous at Pierre's Hole had been a gloomy affair until Sublette's caravan arrived with the liquor. Now it went into full swing, with the Rocky Mountain Fur Company doing all the business as the other traders looked on enviously. The company's clerks got all that was left of their own men's pelts after accounts had been settled and most of the plews of the free trappers, and signed up for the next season a gratifying number of the opposition's men.

Old friends embraced one another enthusiastically, exchanged reminiscences, told tall tales of their winter's adventures, and accounted for companions whose hair had been lifted. The assemblage was thrown into an uproar one day when a big grizzly charged through the camp. The crowd scattered in all directions before him until someone stopped his mad progress with a rifle ball. The Indians bartered their pelts, filled themselves with liquor, sold from their herds the handsome Appaloosa horses bred by the Nez Percés, and altogether added much to the enjoyment of the occasion. On the sporting side, there were contests of skill: wrestling, jumping, foot and horse racing, rifle shooting, and gambling.

Above all, gambling. Indians were inveterate gamblers, as were also the mountain men. Most favored was the "hand game," in which you held your two fists before you, one closely above the other, with a small piece of polished bone concealed in one. Then with various magic incantations, you secretly slid, or pretended to slide, the bone back and forth from one fist to the other. After a little of this mumbo jumbo, you spread your arms far apart, and your opponent guessed which fist held the bone. The men—and sometimes the squaws—would bet their last plew on this game, and then go on to lose their shirts and other garments until they were practically naked.

Gambling sometimes led to violent quarrels, which usually ended in a round of honest fisticuffs followed by maudlin reconciliations. Occasionally there were more serious quarrels, leading to knife play and dangerous or even fatal wounds. It was seldom, however, that a knife was "socked up to the Green River." English hunting knives, the favorite cutlery, were always stamped at the butt of the blade with the initials of the king's Latin title, Georgius

A rendezvous—where old friends embraced one another, told tall tales of the winter's adventures, and gambled with the Indians.

Rex. Mountain men insisted that the letters *GR* stood for "Green River."

In addition to their pelts and horses, the Indians had other merchandise to trade. Trappers would need new moccasins, hunting shirts, and breeches. They would doubtless buy new woolen clothes at the company store, but in the rough work of the fall trapping season cloth garments would not last long. Indian women were skilled in making buckskin garments, which were better for trapping, although they were apt to shrink uncomfortably after becoming wet.

Like beaver pelts, women, whether wives or daughters, were always stock-in-trade. In their younger years, the girls of some tribes were often beautiful and more fastidious in personal cleanliness than most of the frontier white women of the time. Chastity among the women of the Plains tribes was a very rare thing. A handful of beads or other foofaraw was sufficient lure for a casual affair. A semipermanent helpmate was considerably more costly, since the deal was usually negotiated through a middleman, such as a father or current husband.

For an Indian woman, the attention of a white trapper was flattering, and she welcomed a semipermanent arrangement. It enhanced her social status, and she could usually count on better treatment than could be expected from a spouse of her own race. It was a matter of pride with a mountain man to have his woman outshine the others in gaudy adornment. But her position was never secure, for her lord could divorce her as casually as he had married her. If he grew tired of her incessant talking or spied others more beautiful, he simply told her to go back to her father's tepee, and that was that.

Only the gleanings of the rich harvest of the 1832 rendezvous were gathered by the American Fur Company. Their caravan did not come in until most of the customers had gone broke. The Rocky Mountain Company cleaned up. It had been a good trapping year, and at the end of the rendezvous the trains made the eastward march loaded to the limit with beaver.

The standard price paid for pelts at Pierre's Hole was $4 per pound. An average pelt weighed one-and-a-half pounds, making "$6 a plew, prime" the average amount received by the customer in goods—goods at mountain prices. If competition was stiff, the purchase value of an extra-choice pelt might mount to as much as $10.

Merchandise was sold, as always, at a tremendous markup. Whiskey—a spoonful or two of raw alcohol plus a pint of creek water—cost the buyer at least $5; alcohol cost the company from 20 to 25 cents a gallon in St. Louis. For coarse cloth, the trapper paid $10 a yard; for fine cloth, up to $20. These items had cost the company 14 cents a yard for domestic calico, 20 to 35 cents for French calico, and 50 to 90 cents for stroudings and flannels.

Luxuries such as coffee, sugar, and spices sold at a standard price of $2 a pound. In St. Louis coffee was 15 cents a pound; sugar, 9 to 10 cents. Flour, a great and rare luxury purchased by the seller at a little over 2 cents a pound, was sold at $2 a pound in the mountains. Gunpowder and lead, costing 6 to 7 cents a pound, sold at $2 a pound. All these were prices paid by trappers. For the Indian, they would be bargain prices—the simple children of the forest were charged even more. Horses were cheap; you could buy a horse from an Indian for goods costing around $10 in St. Louis.

Some imaginative trapper must have invented the yarn about the mountain method of fixing the price of rifles. As the story goes, rifle barrels were made much longer than necessary in order to boost the price. When you picked the weapon you wanted to buy, the company's clerk stood it on the butt of its stock, and you paid as many plews as were required to make a stack reaching to the muzzle. This is just another tall tale. Barrels were made long in order to get all the range and accuracy possible from old-fashioned black powder. A rifle cost from eight to fourteen pelts, depending on its quality. The old muzzle-loading gun was from four-and-a-half to five-and-a-half feet long, and it would take a lot of pelts to make a stack that high.

Osborne Russell, whose indignation as a trapper may have led to exaggeration, estimated that the fur companies gained an average of 2,000 percent on all goods sold. Company men on salary, as distinguished from free trappers, were paid as much as $1,500 a year if they were skilled in their trade. Free trappers, being generally more energetic and self-reliant, might do better than this if they were lucky in their hunting.

In Pierre's Hole the roistering at last came to an end and the rendezvous began to break up. The first party to set out was led by Bill Sublette's brother Milton. He left on the afternoon of July 17 with a brigade bound for the country north of Great Salt Lake.

They camped for the first night some six or eight miles south of the rendezvous site.

Soon after they started the next morning, a large band of Indians appeared in the distance, and as they drew nearer Milton made them out to be Gros Ventres. That meant a fight. He ordered his men to prepare themselves behind a breastwork of their baggage, and sent two messengers posthaste back to the rendezvous to summon reinforcements. The Indians halted at the base of a hill, broke out a white flag, and sent forward one of their war chiefs carrying a peace pipe. Antoine Godin, a French half-breed, went to meet him for a parley, accompanied by a Flathead chief. Godin's father had recently been murdered by the Gros Ventres, so he had no love for the tribe. He was too familiar with their ways to believe they wanted peace and was sure they had made this move merely to gain time to prepare for battle. As Godin rode up to him, the Gros Ventre chief extended his hand in pretended friendship. The half-breed grasped it and held on firmly while his Flathead companion shot the man dead. They scalped him and dashed back to their own people, carrying his scarlet blanket flapping in the breeze behind them. The enraged Gros Ventres began at once to make a rough breastwork of trees while the squaws dug gun pits behind it.

Bill Sublette, arriving from Pierre's Hole with a strong reinforcement of trappers, Flatheads, and Nez Percés, took command and ordered a charge, the whites to approach the enemy breastwork from one flank and the Indians from the other. The charge was not a success. The only man who reached the breastwork climbed to the top of the logs and immediately fell back, riddled with bullets and arrows. Several others of the attackers were shot down, and Bill Sublette himself was seriously wounded. They carried him back and propped him against a tree, where he continued to give orders. An attempt to burn the enemy out of their fort failed, partly because the Indian allies objected to burning the loot they expected to collect.

After this, both sides settled down to shooting at each other from behind their shelters, tactics that continued for hours without advantage to either. Late in the afternoon, a Gros Ventre shouted from the breastwork that eight hundred more of their warriors were coming soon to end the affair. This threat was misunderstood, the whites taking it to mean that eight hundred Gros Ventres were at that moment looting the undermanned camp at Pierre's Hole. Most of the men immediately rushed off to defend their friends and property, only to find when they got there that everything was as they had left it—no enemy had appeared, nor did any appear during the night.

The next morning, when everybody returned to the field of battle, they found the Gros Ventre fort deserted. The enemy, carrying their wounded, had silently slipped away into the mountains. A count of casualties showed that the trappers had lost twelve killed and thirteen wounded. The losses of the Gros Ventres were never certainly known. They left nine dead in the fort, and later admitted the loss of twenty-six warriors and all their baggage and horses.

The battle of Pierre's Hole, the most severe ever fought between mountain men and Indians in the Rockies, brought the rendezvous of 1832 to an end. All the participants soon pulled out, the supply caravans loaded with beaver pelts for St. Louis, the trapping brigades for the mountain valleys to begin the fall hunt.

From the Mountains to the Sea

During the flush years of the trade, the American Fur Company and the Rocky Mountain Fur Company, the two leading American outfits, by no means had things their own way. The central Rockies were overrun by smaller outfits as well as an increasing number of free trappers, all fighting one another. Without compunction they pirated the furs of rivals, hired away their employees, and egged on the tribes to raid their trapping brigades. They penetrated the most remote mountain valleys, relentlessly trapping out the beavers wherever they went.

At the junction of the Missouri and Yellowstone stood Fort Union, headquarters of the western department of the American

Fur Company, firmly ruled by Kenneth McKenzie. "The King of the Missouri" was a man of education and culture, who lived in luxury and entertained guests with imported wines at his perfectly appointed table.

But when it came to business, he was utterly ruthless. Fort Union was in the heart of the Blackfoot country, and McKenzie had succeeded in doing what no other *bourgeois* had ever done: he had won the allegiance of the tribe that had always been the most bitter enemy of American fur men. The Blackfeet traded their pelts at Fort Union, did not molest its trappers, and often camped outside its stockade. McKenzie did not scruple to sell firearms to these marauders, knowing the weapons would be used against his rivals and hinder them from operating in beaver country that he claimed as his private preserve. He not only supplied the Blackfeet with arms, but undoubtedly encouraged their murderous raids against his competitors.

Federal laws prohibited taking liquor into the Indian country, but scant attention was paid to the regulations. Many government officials used the law merely as a means of exacting bribes from the fur companies. The scandal became so blatant that Congress took notice and forced inspectors to be more honest. Small operators could usually smuggle past inspectors the moderate quantity of alcohol they needed, but the American Fur Company could not hide on riverboats their much larger supply. So McKenzie brought in his own still and began to make alcohol from corn bought from the Mandans.

From Fort Union and other posts that McKenzie built farther up the Missouri, his trapping parties ranged throughout the central Rockies. In addition to his good trading relations with the Blackfeet, he won the trade of the Crows by hiring as his agent Jim Beckwourth, their mulatto war chief, at a yearly salary of eight hundred dollars (Jim in his book makes it three thousand dollars). All this activity was rapidly wiping out the beavers, and the mountain men were again forced to find new hunting grounds farther to the west.

When McKenzie's illegal distillery was at length reported by a disgruntled trapper, the government threatened to revoke his company's trading license, and the scofflaw *bourgeois* was forced to leave the country.

The Hudson's Bay Company and the North West Company, recognizing at last the folly of tearing at each other's throats, had united in 1821 under the name of the older organization. George Simpson, a hard, ruthless driver of men, had become general manager of the merged company, and now that both the great Canadian rivals were under his control he turned against the Americans the old cutthroat tactics they had formerly used against each other. His avowed policy was "Erase the opposition!" Dr. George McLoughlin, a giant of a man both physically and mentally, was made commander of the Columbia River operations.

One of his first moves was to abandon Astoria and build a new post, which he named Fort Vancouver, up the river at the mouth of the Willamette. This location was more convenient to rich beaver country, and the pelts could still be shipped from there on ocean-going vessels. From the new post, McLoughlin's trapping brigades ranged far up the Columbia and its tributaries.

All this country was known as Oregon. Nobody was sure who owned it or how much territory the name included. England and the United States had agreed by treaty that the citizens of both countries should have the right to trap there, and both held that Oregon included the Columbia. McLoughlin was evidently taking steps to occupy the entire watershed of the great river, but by now a few American ranchers had settled along the lower reaches of the Columbia and the Willamette, holding it to be U.S. territory on the strength of Captain Gray's discovery and the Lewis and Clark exploration. Father Junipero Serra, a member of the Franciscan Order, had long since established a chain of missions along the southern coast of California, and Mexico, newly free of Spanish rule, held undisputed possession there. To complicate the situation still further, Russian ships, in search of the marvelously valuable fur of the sea otter, were operating down the coast from their base at Nootka Sound on Vancouver Island. Here were the seeds of international conflict.

George Simpson, the Hudson's Bay Company's new manager, resolved to stop further American advance from the central Rockies by stripping the entire Snake River region bare of beavers. It was hoped that this outrageous tactic would rob the Americans of incentive for going farther west.

Peter Skene Ogden, a rough-and-ready Hudson's Bay *bourgeois*, was sent by Simpson to do the job of extermination. He began his task to the east of Great Salt Lake with a large brigade of whites, half-breeds, and Indians divided into small trapping parties along the Weber River. He had gathered a good haul of pelts when an American brigade ran across some of his Indians and offered them better prices for their fur than Ogden was authorized to pay. Many of them deserted to the Americans, who eventually got most of Ogden's fur and marched away with it after narrowly avoiding a shooting fight.

Ogden's unsuccessful threat did little to deter the restless mountain men, who were always driven by an irresistible urge to have a look at the next valley or around the next river bend. And now they had to face the fact that the mountains were overcrowded with trappers, and no longer provided the rich bounty of former years.

Jedediah Smith had already blazed a trail westward by making two adventure-filled trips to look over the possibilities for trade in California. Smith and his partners, Jackson and Sublette, had bought out Ashley in 1826. Smith then led a party of seventeen trappers from Bear Lake, on the present Idaho-Utah border, across the parched Mohave Desert to the mission of San Gabriel in California. Here they were arrested by the governor for having entered Mexican territory without permission, but were released on promising to return immediately by the same route. Instead of doing this, they went north through the San Joaquin valley, loading their packhorses with beaver skins as they went.

When they reached the base of the Sierra Nevada Mountains, Smith, with only two companions, started back east to report the success of the venture to his partners, leaving the others of his party to guard the furs already taken and to continue trapping. After crossing the Sierras, the three men suffered agonies of hunger and thirst in the deserts of Nevada and western Utah, but finally reached Bear Lake in safety.

Smith made a glowing report to his partners about the wealth of beaver to be found in California, and with only ten days' rest started back with a large brigade of trappers over his old Mohave Desert route. On his first march, he had found the Mohave Indians friendly, but now they suddenly attacked the brigade as it was crossing the Colorado River on rafts. Ten men and most of the supplies were lost, but Smith and eight other survivors fought off the Mohaves and went on afoot.

After a heartbreaking march they arrived at the coast, only to be held up again by the Mexican authorities. The friendly intervention of an American ship captain, who was buying cattle hides on the coast, persuaded the Mexicans to let the party go on. When they had picked up the men and furs left behind at the foot of the Sierra Nevadas, they traveled through northern California into the present state of Oregon.

Bivouacked one evening on the Umpqua River, Smith went out with two men to scout the next day's route. On their return they found the camp a shambles; fifteen men lay dead and all the fur, horses, and baggage had been stolen. Only one man had survived a sudden attack by a band of Umpqua Indians. Smith, his two scouting companions, and the lone survivor of the massacre eventually made it to the newly built Fort Vancouver on the Columbia. Dr. McLoughlin, in command there, extended generous hospitality, and sent out an armed party that recovered most of the stolen property. The hospitable *bourgeois* then bought all of Smith's fur—at a price that was very attractive to the Hudson's Bay Company.

When Smith at last rejoined his partners at Bear Lake, the firm operated successfully until 1830, when they sold out. The handsome profits were invested in the Santa Fe trade, which was in no way concerned with beaver skins. On his first trip from St. Louis to the old Spanish town, Smith got thirsty one day. As he knelt to dig for water in a dry creek bed, a Comanche Indian crept up behind him and ended his adventurous career. He was a man of

fairly good education and deeply religious nature, who carried a
Bible in his pouch as habitually as he carried a rifle in his arms.

The already overcrowded Rocky Mountains were invaded by a
newcomer in the summer of 1832. Captain Benjamin Louis Eulalie
de Bonneville, of French parentage and a graduate of West Point,
was granted a two-year leave from the army to try his hand at
getting rich in the fur trade. In addition to his trapping activities,
he agreed with his army superiors to take careful note of the lay
of the land, and to take with him an experienced man to make
maps. Bonneville's six-cylinder name was too much for the simple
mountain men, and it was soon shortened to "Bald Head."

With ample financial backing, his outfit pulled out from Independence, near St. Louis, with 110 men, the goods and duffle
packed—wonder of wonders—in twenty wagons. Bonneville believed that wheels could roll all the way to the Columbia, and his
wheels did roll a good part of the way.

Eight years before this, William Ashley had taken a small
wheeled cannon up the Platte, which indicated that this route
might be possible for wagon transport, and thousands of immigrant
wagons that later churned the sod of the prairies to dust on the
Oregon Trail proved that this was true. Jed Smith, on returning
from his California adventure, had reported the same possibility.
In 1830 two "carriages" and ten wagons had been taken by the
Platte route to Popo Agie Creek, just short of the Continental
Divide. But no wagons before Bonneville's had crossed the Divide
and gone on west of the mountains.

The use of wagons in place of pack mules cut in half the number
of men and animals required to transport a given amount of
baggage. A mule's pack had to be unloaded at the end of every
day's march and loaded again next morning, but this time-con-
suming labor was not necessary with wagons. Rivers, creeks,
gullies, and mountains made formidable obstacles, to be sure, but
Bonneville won through with his wagons by way of South Pass,
over the Continental Divide, and to west of the Wind River Range
of Wyoming. He made bullboats of his wagon beds by stretching

buffalo hides over them and floated them across Green River. The dry mountain air shrank wheels until the tires dropped off, but an overnight soak in a stream swelled the rims so the iron would hold on for a while.

The Oregon Trail was no boulevard, but Bonneville was no tenderfoot. He had had much frontier experience with the army, and he profited by the expert advice of Joe Walker, his right-hand man, an old hand in the mountains and one of the best.

In western Wyoming at the mouth of Horse Creek on Green River, Bonneville built a post which old trappers nicknamed "Fort Nonsense." From this base and others that he built later, his men ranged far into the Oregon country, and Joe Walker took one party of trappers all the way to California. Everywhere Bonneville met with brutal opposition from the older trading companies and suffered from the usual depredations of the Blackfeet. At the end of a three-year struggle he went broke.

There has always been much speculation as to whether Bonneville was primarily out for beaver, or at least in some way acted as an agent of the United States government to report activities of the British in the Oregon country. He certainly made determined efforts to collect pelts, but this could have been merely a cloak to disguise his real business. He made frequent reports to the U.S. War Department on the Hudson's Bay Company's advance into Oregon, territory that at the time was claimed by both England and the United States. If this dispute had ever led to war, "Fort Nonsense" would have made an ideally situated base for military operations.

But if Bonneville was actually in business for himself, it was also a good base for beaver-trapping, in spite of the contrary opinion of some mountain men. The captain overstayed his leave by almost two years and was dismissed from the army as a consequence, but President Andrew Jackson, a rigid old soldier, promptly reinstated him in spite of this serious breach of discipline. No positive evidence has ever come to light as to whether or not he was sent out as a spy.

A further addition to the overpopulation of the mountains was made in 1832, when Nathaniel J. Wyeth arrived with his outfit at the Pierre's Hole rendezvous. Wyeth was a shrewd Yankee ice dealer from Cambridge, Massachusetts, who had come west with a new scheme.

Planning to set himself up in the Oregon fur trade, he had sent a shipload of supplies from Boston to the Columbia, which greatly reduced the expense of land transportation. When his ship was well on her way, he set out overland from Independence, Missouri, with a party of trappers. He would meet the ship at the Columbia and establish himself in the fur business there with the trade goods she had brought. The crew would then catch and salt down a load of salmon, pick up any pelts Wyeth might have gathered, and sell this rich cargo in Boston. This, he hoped, would pay the expense of the entire sea voyage. Wyeth himself intended to stay on permanently as a trader.

With his group of two dozen enthusiasts, he left Independence under the protection of the Rocky Mountain Fur Company supply train, which was bound for the rendezvous at Pierre's Hole. His outfit included, among more conventional equipment, gaudy uniforms for the men, bayonets for their rifles, three boats on wheels for use on either land or water, as well as ten bugles to enliven the trip. Much of this impractical baggage was later discarded along the trail.

Wyeth proved to be extremely apt at learning mountain craft, and was by no means a tenderfoot by the time he arrived at the rendezvous. He underwent his baptism of fire at the battle of Pierre's Hole, where he gave such a good account of himself that he earned the respect of the old hands. For half his party the battle quenched the thirst for adventure, and they went back to St. Louis with the returning fur caravans. But not Nat Wyeth. He and the few other stalwarts went on to the Columbia, traveling with one of the trapping brigades until they were beyond danger of attack by the Blackfeet.

On reaching Fort Vancouver, Wyeth was made welcome and spent the winter there, a stay marred by the tragic news that his ship from Boston had gone down at sea with all her cargo. When spring came, he went back to the mountains, where he succeeded in making a deal to furnish supplies for the next summer's Rocky Mountain Fur Company rendezvous. Going back to Boston, this determined bankrupt raised new capital, bought a stock of trade goods at St. Louis, and made the long march west to Green River, only to be met with a refusal by the Rocky Mountain partners to honor their contract. Their excuse was that the trapping season had been a poor one, and they already had enough stock on hand to serve their customers.

In bitter mood, Wyeth went on west with the unsold goods and built a post, Fort Hall, on the Snake. Leaving a few men here in the hope—which proved vain—that the supplies could be sold to local Indians, he again headed for Fort Vancouver, where he spent the next summer trapping on the Columbia and Willamette. A second ship which he had sent out from Boston was struck by lightning at sea and spent three months being refitted at Valparaiso, Chile. He had intended to have her return to Boston with a cargo of salted salmon, but she arrived too late for the annual spawning run. A ship that he sent from the Columbia to the Sandwich Islands (Hawaii) with a cargo of lumber returned to report no profits.

After four years of unmerited disasters, Wyeth finally had to acknowledge that he was at the end of his rope. He sold Fort Hall to the Hudson's Bay Company and went home to Cambridge, where he resumed his ice business. By shipping New England ice to the West Indies, he at last won prosperity. After all the body blows that fate had dealt him, he deserved it.

On his second trip to the Rockies, Wyeth, by then a full-fledged mountain man, acted as guide and counselor to Jason Lee, first of the many missionaries who went west with fur company caravans during the next few years to attempt the tough job of christianizing the Indians. Lee was accompanied by four lay assistants and two milk cows.

The Rev. Jason Lee was a man of deep piety. He firmly believed that Divine Providence constantly intervened in all life's small affairs. In his view, the appearance of a buffalo herd when the party with which he traveled needed meat, the chance finding of a stream when they wanted water, a violent storm that prevented desecration of the Lord's Day by making a Sunday march impossible, all these were evidences of the concern of the Almighty in the success of his mission. He had been sent out by the Methodist Church to minister to the Flatheads, but wound up far away from them on the Willamette. Here he and his four companions, among the first Americans who crossed the continent to establish homesteads, joined a few fellow countrymen who had come to Oregon by sea.

Under Lee's vigorous leadership the colony staked out farms and planted crops that flourished mightily in the fertile soil of the Willamette valley. He went back east to deliver a series of lectures

Americans began to cross the continent to establish homesteads, staking out farms and planting crops.

that attracted many other homesteaders, and the population increased to a point where it aroused the concern of Dr. McLoughlin
at Fort Vancouver, who did not view with satisfaction the settlement of his beaver-trapping territory by farmers. This successful
colony set the pattern for the great migration. In the next few
years, thousands of settlers would reach the promised land under
the guidance of fur trappers.

Jason Lee was soon followed by other missionaries, all of whom
traveled most of the way under the protection of fur company
caravans. Without exception, they were brave, consecrated men
who were filled with zeal, but they had no experience of the hard
lives they must lead, and little understanding of the Stone Age
people to whom they attempted to explain the mysteries of Christianity. They met many discouragements, and had some fantastic adventures.

One of the most notable of these good men was Dr. Marcus
Whitman, a medical missionary, who went out to establish a
mission for the Flatheads and Nez Percés, tribes that had sent a
delegation to St. Louis to ask for instruction in the white man's
religion. Whitman made two trips to the mountains, the first to
look over the ground and select a site for his mission, the second to
bring out equipment and personnel.

On his first journey, traveling with the American Fur Company's supply train, he proved his worth. One night when the
caravan was camped on the Missouri, Lucien Fontenelle, its commander, roused him out of his blankets to treat one of the men who
had suddenly collapsed. Whitman recognized the symptoms at
once: the man had Asiatic cholera. By morning the dread disease
had struck down several others. Though ill and exhausted himself,
Whitman battled the epidemic for twelve days and nights, practically without sleep. Before running its course, the disease
claimed three victims and left many convalescents, but the doctor
had prevented the scourge from wiping out the entire caravan.

At Fort Laramie, Tom Fitzpatrick took over the weakened party
from Fontenelle and led it to the rendezvous at the mouth of New
Fork on the Green River. Here the doctor had his first experience of

the freewheeling festivities of a mountain trading fair, and took part as the star in a special event. In a brush with the Blackfeet three years before, Jim Bridger's back had stopped two arrows. He managed to pull one of them out, but the shaft of the other broke off and he had been carrying the point around ever since. It bothered him some, so he consulted Whitman for professional advice. As the whole camp looked on with fascinated interest, the doctor performed his first operation as a medical missionary. The barbed arrowhead was made of iron, and the point had bent around one of the patient's bones, but Whitman's skill was equal to the occasion. He butchered out the arrow, and made a lifelong friend of Jim Bridger. The doctor expressed amazement that this large foreign substance, embedded so long in the flesh, had not caused blood poisoning. "Doctor," said Jim, "in this cool mountain air, meat don't spoil."

With this experience behind him, Whitman was no greenhorn on his second trip the following summer. Again he traveled with an American Fur Company train commanded by Tom Fitzpatrick, headed for the rendezvous on Horse Creek, a tributary of the Green. He was accompanied by the bride he had just married, and by the Rev. Henry Spalding and his wife. Eliza Spalding and Narcissa Whitman were making history by being the first white women to brave the perils of an overland journey to the Rocky Mountains. Spalding, while entirely sincere in his religious profession, was a solemn, narrow-minded zealot, and his wife, a dour, sad-eyed woman with little charm. Narcissa was a decided contrast to her. A vivacious strawberry blonde and a bit of a coquette, she was adored by the dazzled mountain men, as well as by the awestruck Indians.

No full measure of Christian brotherhood existed between the two couples. Spalding had been in love with Narcissa long before she knew Whitman, but she had spurned his suit. Smarting under the necessity of traveling with her as the wife of another, and intolerant of any behavior that did not accord with his own narrow views, he now attempted to change her lighthearted gaiety to the degree of decorum he considered proper for the wife of a missionary. Eliza Spalding shared her husband's disapproval of Narcissa, and the two of them made life difficult for her. Whitman resented their censure of his bride, so the relationship of the four did not abound in mutual goodwill.

From the rendezvous, the missionaries went on to the Nez Percé country with a Hudson's Bay brigade and founded two missions—one, with Whitman in charge, among the Cayuse Indians on the Walla Walla River; the other, under Spalding, some seventy-five miles away to serve the Nez Percés and Flatheads. At these posts the two devoted men struggled for eleven years. They had moderate success in their work, and by 1847 appeared to be well established in the good graces of their charges. Then disaster struck.

While some few of the Cayuses had acquired a veneer of Christianity, they still looked upon Dr. Whitman as a superior type of sorcerer who, like their own medicine men, might work evil magic against them at any time. Emigrants had begun to make the Whitman mission a stopping place for rest on their way farther west.

In the fall of 1847, a wagon train stopped in which there was a case of measles. This usually mild malady spread like wildfire through the mission, and before it had run its course proved fatal to more than half the tribe, who had no built-up resistance to it. The superstitious Cayuses ascribed all their troubles to the sorcery of Dr. Whitman. They were sure now that he was working evil magic against them, for no whites had died—only their own people. As the doctor sat reading by the fire one day, an Indian crept up behind him and sank a tomahawk in his skull.

A bloody massacre followed, in which Narcissa Whitman, eleven men, and two children lost their lives, and all the other whites were carried away as captives. When news of the tragedy reached Fort Vancouver, a rescue party was sent out which succeeded in ransoming the survivors, among whom was the little daughter of Jim Bridger, who had been sent by her father to be educated by Narcissa. Joe Meek, Bridger's friend, had also placed a daughter in her care, and Helen Mar Meek was among the victims.

Long before the Walla Walla mission met its tragic end, other wives of missionaries had followed Narcissa Whitman and Eliza Spalding. In the summer of 1838, two trappers arriving at a spot on Horse Creek that had been set for the rendezvous found only a message scrawled on the door of a shack. It read: "Come on to Popoasia. Plenty of whiskey and white women." They went on to the junction of the Popo Agie and Wind River, where they found the tents, trading booths, and horse herds of the American Fur Company, the usual crowd of roisterers—and, as advertised, four white women. They and their missionary husbands were bound for the Whitman mission on the Walla Walla.

Two of them, Mary Walker and Myra Eels, kept diaries in which they recorded with monotonous regularity the bickerings and quarrels indulged in by the four couples during their journey. At the Popo Agie rendezvous, the ladies were subjected to considerable annoyance by the unregenerate mountain men, due partly to the availability of strong drink, but mostly to their excitement at seeing white squaws for the first time in many years.

The women busied themselves with a frenzy of clothes-washing and bread-baking, using flour they had brought with them. Bread was a rare delicacy for these men who lived almost exclusively on meat, and they found numerous tasks that would keep them busy near the bake oven while they reveled in the entrancing fumes. Wheat flour was too precious an article for the ladies to feed everybody, so fumes were all the bread-hungry trappers got.

Joe Meek, however, was more resourceful than most. Tormented beyond endurance by the tantalizing odors, he devised a scheme. He saw Mary Walker reward an Indian for singing a gospel hymn by giving him a freshly baked biscuit. Joe was no good at singing hymns, but he prevailed on the Indian to go back and sing another, for which Mary gave him the same reward. As the vocalist carried the prize away, Joe fell upon him in the woods, hijacked the biscuit, and enjoyed his first taste of hot bread in nine years.

Traveling always under the protection of trappers, the four couples reached Dr. Whitman's mission at the end of August,

1838. Along the way, a pregnant squaw neared her time. With some anxiety Mrs. Walker noted in her diary: "Conner's squaw just about to give birth. Can't move camp on account of the horses." After rounding up the horse herd, they went on. For two days the expectant mother kept pace with the caravan, riding astride. On the third day she fell behind, "following the camp about thirty miles. At noon she collected fuel and prepared dinner. Gave birth to a daughter about sunset." The next day, "the squaw came into camp about ten with the child in her arms, smart as could be."

V

SUNSET OF
THE MOUNTAIN MEN

End of the Golden Harvest

WE HAVE SEEN HOW JOHN JACOB ASTOR FORMED
an alliance with the Chouteaus, the St. Louis fur barons, after his
agents sold Fort Astoria to the Nor'westers. This alliance, with
headquarters at St. Louis, invaded the Rockies in bitter and well-
financed competition with the other outfits that operated there.
Their chief rival, the Rocky Mountain Fur Company, fought back
with equally ruthless tactics. Price-cutting, pirating one another's
furs, bribery of brigade leaders, encouragement of Indian raids
against rivals, even murder, became commonplace practices of the
trade. Gruesome evidence of the murder of rival trappers was dis-
guised so it would appear to be the result of Indian raids. With
Astor's financial backing his outfit, the American Fur Company,
won out in this lawless warfare, and their chief rival finally went
bankrupt.

In 1834 Astor, now grown fabulously wealthy, sold out to his
associates. Beavers were steadily getting scarcer and scarcer, prices
were on the downgrade, and he foresaw an end to the golden
harvest. He would let his former partners take the risks while he
reaped a sure profit as their banker.

From London he wrote one of his associates: "I fear that beaver
will not sell very well unless very fine. It appears they make hats
out of silk in place of beaver." One story has it that a foppish
French nobleman traveling in China lost his beaver hat, and unable
to find another that he fancied, ordered a new one to be made of
silk. The style spread throughout the world of fashion till every

man with any pretense to elegance coveted one like it. An added body blow to the beaver hunters was the invention of machinery that made fairly good felt from less expensive furs, such as rabbit, nutria, seal, and cat.

Astor, always a man of remarkable foresight, had foreseen the trend which within a few years made itself felt in the mountains. The demand for beaver fell off and the price of pelts plummeted. In 1832 plews brought $6 per pound in St. Louis; by 1833 the price had dropped to $3.50, and it continued to drop steadily afterward. Such prices robbed the trade of its profits.

At the time when Dr. Whitman rescued Fontenelle's supply caravan from Asiatic cholera, the disease attacked the tribes of the upper Missouri, and many deaths occurred. Francis Chardon, Indian-hating *bourgeois* at Fort Clark on the Missouri above the Mandan towns, expressed discontent in his journal over the small number of deaths at his post; he would have been glad to see all the Indians wiped out. Recording the departure of a Mandan war party to attack the Sioux, he makes this pious entry: "God send them speed. It is perfectly immaterial how few of them return. I wish both parties a severe conflict and heavy losses."

Chardon's wishes were gratified in short order. In the middle of June, 1837, the steamboat *St. Peter's* came up the river (steamboats were now the usual means of transporting supplies on the Missouri). At Fort Clark she unloaded a consignment of goods— and with it, a consignment of death. During her voyage up the river, several cases of smallpox had broken out among the crew, and while she was tied up at the Fort Clark dock an Indian stole a blanket that had been used by one of the victims. Less than a month later, a young Mandan died of smallpox, and from then on the disease swept through the tribe like a windblown prairie fire through dry grass. The Mandans were convinced that the *bourgeois* at Fort Clark had cursed them through black magic. They made several attempts to murder Chardon, and the garrison was obliged to maintain a state of siege to avoid being massacred.

The Sioux, taking advantage of the weakened condition of the Mandans, raided their villages, and the returning warriors carried the fatal contagion to their own people. The scourge spread to the Arikaras, the Assiniboins, the Blackfeet, and Minnetarees. Many despairing Indians committed suicide. Before the epidemic died out among the Mandans, only thirty-one of the populous tribe of sixteen hundred were left alive. In their villages the only sounds to be heard were the croaking of ravens and the howling of wolves. Many other tribes were reduced to mere remnants of their former strength. At a conservative estimate, fifteen thousand Indians died, a tremendous percentage of the population affected by the epidemic.

Chardon, in summing up this fearful tragedy, writes, "What a band of RASCALS has been used up." Such a comment is not only evidence of the heartless callousness with which many fur men viewed Indians; it is also evidence of a lack of understanding of what was good for their own interests. The effects of the smallpox epidemic on the fur trade became evident at the next rendezvous, where the few Indian customers who had the heart to attend brought only a pitifully small supply of pelts.

Not only were there few Indians left to hunt the beaver; there were few beaver left for them to hunt. The times were past when a man could find good trapping in almost any stream. The far-ranging mountain men had cleaned their quarry out of every creek and brook. The "strip the country bare" policy of the Hudson's Bay Company, though it had failed where Peter Skene Ogden tried it at Great Salt Lake, had been effective in other places. The area between the Rockies and the Snake was cleaned out. In 1826 the Hudson's Bay harvest in this region had been more than 2,000 pelts; by 1835 it had dropped to 220.

The lush old days were no more. The trading fair held on Horse Creek in the summer of 1839 was the last real rendezvous, and it was only a parody of those of former years. A cloud of gloom hung over the gathering, and the carefree revels of the great days were nowhere in evidence. Black Harris, a leather-faced old-timer, brought out a much smaller caravan than had been customary, with only a meager supply of liquor, but the men did not seem to mind very much; they were too downhearted to feel like cele-brating.

With Harris' supply train came a few missionaries, as well as an omen of what was soon to come—a sprinkling of homesteaders who intended to settle permanently in the rich farming country beyond the Rockies. Oregon fever was becoming epidemic in the East, and in the rude frontier settlements of Independence and Westport, near present-day Kansas City, the vanguard of the great migration was beginning to gather. The streets of the two towns were cluttered with piles of equipment: tents, wagons, food, furniture, farming tools. Corrals of mules, horses, and oxen stood near the blacksmith shops, where the music of ringing anvils mingled with the shouts of teamsters, the loud talk of emigrants, trappers, and Indians, the raucous braying of mules, and the barking of innumerable dogs. The crowds of restless "movers" were getting ready to start on the long trek across the prairies and over the mountains to new homes in the fabled lands of the Far West. They would follow the beaver trappers' trails, which by now had been churned into rough roads by the wheels of the fur company caravans.

Most of these movers were staunch frontier people going west with their families in the hope of making better lives for themselves. Some were restless misfits, never content to stay very long in any one place. Among them also were a few of the dregs of the frontier, who had perhaps found it necessary to escape the restraints of law and order. Thousands of movers, goading the plodding oxen that pulled their overloaded wagons, would make their way slowly westward on the Oregon Trail during the coming years, quarreling, splitting into smaller groups, deposing their leaders and choosing new ones, fighting off the Indians whose hunting grounds they were invading, but persevering always in their determination to reach the land of their dreams. The fainthearts fell by the wayside, or turned back disheartened by the hardships of the trail, but those of good courage reached their destinations, to establish homesteads and become leaders in bringing civilization to the Pacific Coast.

Among the first to be attacked by Oregon fever was a group of citizens of Peoria, Illinois, in whom the Rev. Jason Lee, on his lecture tour to gather recruits for the Willamette colony, had awakened an overpowering urge to go west. Calling themselves the Oregon Dragoons and flying a banner reading "Oregon or the Grave," they set out nineteen strong from Westport in the spring of 1839. The usual difficulties marked their progress, but none of them reached the grave on this journey. Some of the fainthearts turned back, but most of the party finally reached Oregon.

From this time on, the emigrant trains grew longer and longer until the migration reached its peak in 1843. From the backwoods farms of the frontier came thousands of restless men and women, dissatisfied with their hard lot and bewitched by shining visions of the fabled lands beyond the Rockies. In Oregon and California, they believed, no blizzards would ever devastate their crops and no impassable roads would hinder carrying their produce to market. They had been told that the black soil of the promised land was bottomless, crops were unbelievably rich, and countless rivers furnished easy transportation. Between 1841 and 1846, more than ten thousand homesteaders in high hope followed the Oregon Trail to the new country.

James K. Polk was elected President in 1844 on a platform that called for the annexation of the newly established Republic of Texas, if its citizens so desired. They voted that they did so desire, and Mexico broke off diplomatic relations with the United States. One of Polk's campaign slogans had been "Fifty-four forty or fight," a threat that his administration would declare war on England unless she agreed to 54°40′ (the latitude of the southern tip of Alaska) as the northern boundary of Oregon. War with Mexico was imminent, and a war with England at the same time was unthinkable.

Polk settled with the British government for a boundary along the 49th parallel from Puget Sound eastward to Lake of the Woods—not by any means all the territory the campaign orators had been shouting for, but a compromise that settled the long-standing boundary dispute. This arrangement left the Columbia River well within the United States, which was a principal point of contention. In the same year the war with Mexico came to a head, an unequal contest that resulted in the annexation of Texas and the highway robbery of all Mexico's possessions in California.

The entire Pacific Coast from the present southern border of California up to Puget Sound was now a part of the United States, and international wrangling as to who owned what territory and who had the right to trap where came to an end. The course of empire had made its way westward to the Pacific; manifest destiny had manifested itself.

As emigrant trains of the great migration continued to raise clouds of dust over the Oregon Trail, a substantial addition was made to the population of the West by the Mormon exodus. Hounded by persecution from one resting place to another east of the Mississippi, this band of zealots followed Brigham Young, their leader, out of Nauvoo, Illinois, to a new Zion on the shores of Great Salt Lake, where they hoped to be left undisturbed in the practice of their religion.

Young had not decided on an exact location for his sanctuary until the first group of his people had gone through South Pass. There he met Jim Bridger, who had quit beaver-hunting and was running a way station for immigrants. On the advice of this master geographer, Young fixed on the country bordering the southeast shores of Salt Lake as the future home of his followers. Other Mormons soon joined the pioneers, and within a few years these steadfast people turned an inhospitable desert into a community of prosperous farms.

Finally, in 1848, gold was discovered in California. During the next year, more than a hundred thousand men, the lust for gold shining in their eyes, came hurrying across the prairies. Where the fur hunters had roamed the mountains and valleys in solitude a few years back, they now ran into interlopers on every march, and so few beavers were left in the streams that trapping was no longer worthwhile.

The Taming of the Wild Men

With this spate of people, the day of the mountain man was over, and he was forced to look for another sort of job. Now that the beaver was nearly exterminated, many turned to the extermination of the buffalo, a task that would have seemed impossible to those who had known the large herds that blanketed the plains in earlier days. The wholesale slaughter of these magnificent animals for their tongues and hides increased steadily from 1834, the first year when the value of the total take of buffalo hides equaled that of beaver. The American bison would have completely disappeared if a few animals that were kept privately on ranches and at the Bronx Zoo in New York had not been drawn upon for breeding. Under strict Government protection in Yellowstone and other federal parks, the buffalo has taken a new lease on life, and there are now several large herds thriving on their old feeding grounds in the West.

Many of the jobless trappers eked out a living as guides for emigrant trains, composing the quarrels of the movers, protecting them from perils of the trail, and leading them in resisting the attacks of hostile Indians. Some of the best mountain men became scouts for the army, which was engaged for years in cowing the desperate tribes whose hunting ranges had been overrun by settlers. During the Indian wars of the 1850's and 1860's, many a commander of Government troops owed the success of his campaign—or the escape of his men from massacre—to the wise counsels of Jim Bridger, Kit Carson, and other old-timers. Carson rose to the rank of brigadier general in the Civil War. In May of 1864, with 325 soldiers, he defeated a thousand hostile Indians at the battle of Adobe Walls in the Texas Panhandle.

Joe Meek settled down as a respectable citizen of Oregon. In the wake of the massacre at the Whitman mission, the aroused Oregonians circulated a petition demanding that the Federal Government organize their area as a United States territory and give it some degree of military protection. Meek, who was a cousin of President Polk's wife, made a dangerous winter journey to Washington to present the petition to Congress. Always ready for a joke, he arrived dressed in greasy buckskins and announced himself as "Envoy Extraordinary and Ambassador Plenipotentiary from the Republic of Oregon to the Court of the United States." Controversy as to whether Oregon should be slave or free-soil

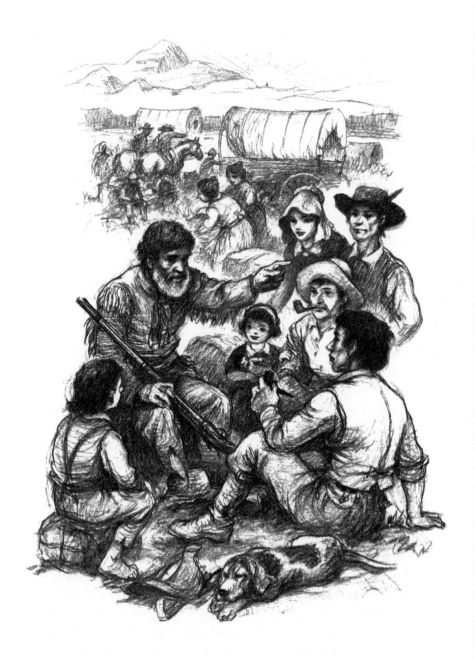

Many jobless trappers found a way to earn a living as guides for emigrant trains.

country held up action by Congress until 1848, when status as a free-soil territory was granted. A governor was appointed, and Meek, who was made U.S. marshal, triumphantly escorted him to his new post.

A few of the more literate mountain men served as officers of the Bureau of Indian Affairs, where they brought intimate knowledge of Indians and genuine concern for their welfare to a service that has not always been noted for such qualities. Some of the older trappers could not change to new ways, and went completely native. With their Indian wives, they lived permanently with their adopted people, in some cases even joining them in raids against the settlers.

A few mountain men acquired a certain sort of fame through the highly imaginative writings of such authors as Ned Buntline and his ilk. Clad in immaculate white buckskins astride well-groomed pinto ponies, these "scouts" shot down glass balls and fought mock battles with tame Indians in the circus ring, much to the delight of tenderfoot small fry.

Jim Beckwourth's ghost-written autobiography tells some gaudy tall tales about his life after the beaver-trapping days were over. He writes that remorse over his unregenerate years as a Crow chieftain drove him to a yearning for civilization, and he moved to St. Louis, leaving his bevy of doting wives to languish among their own people.

In St. Louis he recruited a company of rangers and led them to fight under Colonel Zachary Taylor in a campaign against the Seminole Indians of Florida. After this "war" he turned up in California, where he joined in an unsuccessful rebellion against the local Spanish government. When the war with Mexico began, he stole a thousand horses and drove them (presumably without assistance) to join General Stephen Kearny's army in New Mexico. Jim's exploits in this war, as he tells them, are much too heroic to be believed. One gathers from his own account that his single-handed efforts were largely responsible for the war's successful outcome. With these adventures behind him, the old warrior, suffering the aftermath of numerous wounds, settled down in California to run a cattle ranch and cater to the needs of hungry immigrants. Finally, while on a visit to an encampment of Crow Indians, he suddenly died. Among his old trapping cronies, it was believed that he was poisoned by the people among whom he had lived for so many years.

Jim Bridger, having served for a time as emigrant guide and army scout, again took up trapping in partnership with Louis Vasquez, known among his friends as "Old Vaskiss." But there was too little fur in the beaver-stripped mountains and there were too many silk hats back east. The partners gave up beaver-trapping, and built Fort Bridger, a place of rest, refreshment, and refitting for the emigrant trains. This roadside caravansary, on the Oregon Trail in the southwestern corner of Wyoming, was no Grand Palace Hotel, but it was a very welcome stopping place, a sort of halfway house where travelers could lie up for a few days, wash their clothes, buy supplies, have their animals shod, their wagons repaired, and their courage revived. The best possible advice as to the road ahead and the dangers to be avoided was given without charge.

Bridger did not get along very well with the nearby Mormons. Neither did the Mormons get along very well with the U.S. Government. Their quarrels with unwanted officials sent out from Washington finally led to open rebellion, and in the course of the dispute the rebels burned Fort Bridger to the ground. Jim sold the land to the Government for use as an army post, and again entered the service as a scout. In the Powder River expedition against the Sioux in 1865, he held the rank of chief of scouts. He won high praise from his commander in that campaign, and later retired, old and half blind, to a small farm that he owned near Kansas City.

For the mountain man, the sun had set. The American, French, and British trappers had relentlessly pursued the beaver westward from the Gulf of St. Lawrence to the Pacific Ocean, destroying the raw material of their craft as they went. Theirs was a hard, perilous calling. Every march was attended by danger; every campsite might prove to be their last. Constantly on the move, bedding down under the stars wherever night overtook them, often

wet, cold, and hungry, a year of incessant toil might bring as its
reward no more than a wild spree and enough equipment to embark
on another year of toil.

In many trappers, such a life developed self-reliance, courage,
independence, and skill in overcoming the hazards that were a part
of their trade. In others, freedom from the restraints of civilized
life led to a relapse into near savagery. Whatever may have been
his individual character, the beaver trapper was not a builder—he
was a destroyer. We have followed these men in their march across
the continent as they stripped bare one hunting ground after
another until the beaver was nearly reduced to extinction. This is a
sad spectacle for all who cherish unspoiled wilderness and care for
the preservation of the wild creatures that inhabit it.

But in spite of the destructive character of the beaver trapper's
trade, and the cruelty he necessarily practiced against his victims,
he made a mighty contribution to the winning of the West. In no
way did he look upon himself as a nation builder; he was a simple,
practical man pursuing a trade that provided no more than a bare
living for most of those who followed it. But whether conscious of it
or not, the fur trapper was a man of destiny, the vanguard of
civilization's march across America. The rivers he followed, the
mountains he scaled, the trails he blazed led the westering restless
have-nots and adventurers from the colonies along North America's
Atlantic Coast into a trackless wilderness of white water, green
forests, endless plains and snowcapped mountains in pursuit of
farm land, timber, graze and gold. Quite unknowingly, he broke
the trails that marked the outlines of the American Republic. The
trapper was the spark plug of a great migration that has trans-
formed a wild, trackless wilderness into a land of law and order.
His deeds made history, and he deserves a generous share of the
fame that has been accorded more spectacular heroes.

A New Lease on Life

Any estimate of the beaver population of North America at the time of the white man's coming must be a pure guess.
According to Harold A. Innis, a distinguished Canadian authority,

it has been estimated that there were ten million. Ernest Thompson
Seton's guess is at least sixty million. All we can say with sureness
is that every creek and pond where there was sufficient food had its
quota of lodges. The Hudson's Bay Company alone handled more
than three million pelts during the years from 1853 to 1877,
which was well after the peak period, and they were only one of
many fur companies, free trappers, and Indians who were busy at
the work of wiping out the beaver from the time of the earliest
bartering for pelts on the St. Lawrence.

In 1823 an inventive ironmonger named Sewell Newhouse had
made important improvements in the steel trap at his shop in
Oneida, N.Y. This was bad news for the beaver, but for the trapper
the new contrivance made it possible to take more pelts than could
be taken with the clumsy and inefficient traps that had been
hammered out by blacksmiths with little improvement for centuries.

In time, the Newhouse trap became the favorite model all over
the fur country, and its greater efficiency soon became evident.
Old records show such scores as 250 pelts taken by one man in two
weeks; 155 pelts in one day by a party of twenty men; 5,000 in
one season by twenty trappers. Prices paid by buyers at rendezvous varied from time to time, but an average can be set at $4
per pound. A pelt weighed from one to two pounds, say 80 pelts to
a pack of one hundred pounds, which brought the seller $400. If a
trapper averaged three catches a day through the season, he would
earn about $16 a day. Back east, a farmhand's wage was around
fifty cents a day with board. It is no wonder that so many enterprising young men with a taste for adventure took to beaver-
trapping. To the farmhand, such a reward for his time seemed a
fortune, but he usually failed to balance his earnings against the
ruinous prices he had to pay the fur companies, his only source of
supply. Most newcomers soon fell into the habits of the old-timers,
and blew their season's take at the yearly trading fair.

By 1900, the fur hunters had about completed their task of
extermination. Much earlier than this, beavers had practically
disappeared from the eastern United States, and the situation in

southern Canada, the Rocky Mountains, and the Far West came to the same pass in the last decade of the century. At this low ebb of beaver fortunes, various states began to take steps to rescue the species by outlawing beaver-trapping altogether and importing new stock from places where a few colonies were still hanging on to life.

The experience of New York State in restocking may be taken as an example of what happened all over the country. In the early years of the present century, a few dozen pairs of beavers were introduced into the Adirondack forests, where a survey by the state game department had shown that only a pitiful remnant of the original stock remained. By 1915 these first plantings had increased to an estimated fifteen thousand animals. Under complete protection, beavers multiplied so rapidly that landowners began to complain of damage to their timber, and surplus animals had to be transferred to new locations.

Then a short yearly trapping season was established. An open trapping season now occurs each spring. Decisions about the length of season, dates of opening and closing, number of animals to be taken, and other restraints vary from year to year, and are based on the conditions shown by frequent surveys. Surveys are made from the air. Planes cruise over beaver country and they carry observers who count the lodges that have good caches near them. Old lodges that have been abandoned will have no food caches, so this method results in a reasonably accurate count. By adjusting the bag limit for any open season to the result of such a survey, the beaver population can be kept within limits of the food supply and still leave plenty of breeding stock to carry on. Seven open seasons in New York up to 1940 yielded 22,000 pelts, worth $374,000. Many states now have yearly trapping seasons, and the total value of the pelts taken increases steadily. Under proper controls, trappers are satisfied and the beavers continue to flourish.

The rescue of the beaver, which now seems to be assured, is welcomed by all those who love the outdoors and have an interest in the preservation of wildlife. Most owners of country places are delighted to have beavers move into streams on their property, and do not resent the loss of a few trees around the pond. But the revival of this handsome fur bearer does not meet with entire approval in some quarters. In farming country, beavers can be a nuisance. They pay no attention to "Keep Out" signs. They destroy valuable trees, both by felling them and by drowning their roots, and water backed up by their dams sometimes covers fields where crops are growing. Highway culverts may be clogged with masses of small limbs, resulting in flooded roads after heavy rainfall.

To consider the beaver a pest is of course the farmer's way of looking at it, and undoubtedly he has a point. It does leave its mark upon the land. Tearing out a dam does little to prevent the harm it may cause. The builders, upholding their reputation for eagerness, will repair minor damage overnight, and rebuild a totally destroyed dam in a short time.

But in a broader view, the return of the beaver has resulted in far more good than harm. Many a lush streamside meadow marks the site of an ancient beaver dam. The pond that once stood above it was abandoned long ago when its occupants had used up all the trees near the banks. The pond has filled up solidly with rich silt and now supports growing crops, grazing cattle, or new forest growth. Over the centuries, the face of our land has probably been altered more by the works of beavers than by the works of man, even with his violent urge to push the landscape around with bull-dozers and steam shovels.

The entire character of many watersheds has been altered for the better by the presence of a colony of these busy rodents. As a concrete example of how beavers can benefit a "dead" watershed, let us imagine a burned-out valley, perhaps in the far Northwest, where a settler, hoping to support his family partly by trapping, takes up land along the upper reaches of a stream that has formerly watered the valley. His farm has been granted him free by the state because nobody else wants it. But this man has imagination and thinks he can do something about reclaiming these useless acres.

Great forest fires, burning repeatedly over the ages, have destroyed most of the vegetation. Rainwater, unchecked by the hindering roots of growing plants, has washed away the topsoil of the forest floor. The creek, a raging torrent after heavy rainfall, becomes a series of shallow pools during any dry spell. Between the stagnant pools, there is only a feeble flow. The beavers that once lived here have deserted the area and their untended dams have long since been swept away by floods. Hardly any fish or other aquatic life remain in the water. Moose and deer, browsing animals, shun the area because of the scarcity of foliage. The fields of farmers far down the valley are flooded by the creek after rain and parched at other times, for their irrigation ditches, formerly filled from the stream, have run dry. The entire watershed is steadily becoming a desert.

A resourceful landowner releases in the creek a pair of beavers, furnished him by the state game department. Over a period of a few years, their offspring have made themselves at home. At no cost to the taxpayers, they build dams that serve as catch basins for rain and form deep pools in the headwaters. Plant life again flourishes along the banks and spreads through the moist earth of the forest floor. Heavy rainfall, instead of running off in flood, sinks into the ground and seeps into the creek slowly. Because of this, the current maintains a steady flow, instead of alternating between flood and trickle. Mayflies again drop into the water their tiny eggs, which hatch into flying insects to feed the trout that again find living conditions to their liking and spawn in the pools. Deer and moose return to browse on the foliage along the bank and stand up to their withers in the beaver ponds to protect their hides from insect pests. A generous and steady supply of water now fills the irrigation ditches, and farmers' crops flourish. And the man who, with the help of a pair of beavers, has brought this about harvests a profitable return from his traplines.

Life has returned to a dead watershed. Such renewals of worthless land have occurred again and again all over our country. This is certainly worth a few felled trees and a few acres covered by beaver ponds.

BIBLIOGRAPHY

American Heritage, *Westward on the Oregon Trail*. New York: American Heritage Publishing Co., Inc., 1962.

——, *The Great West*. New York: American Heritage Publishing Co., Inc., 1965.

Bonner, T. D. (ed.), *The Life and Adventures of James P. Beckwourth*. New York: 1856. Alfred A. Knopf, Inc., 1931.

Campbell, Walter Stanley, *Mountain Men*. Boston: Houghton Mifflin Company, 1937.

Chittenden, Hiram M., *The American Fur Trade of the Far West*. Stanford, Calif.: Academic Reprints, 1954.

Cleland, Robert Glass, *This Reckless Breed of Men*. New York: Alfred A. Knopf, Inc., 1950.

Collier, Eric, *Three Against the Wilderness*. New York: E. P. Dutton & Co., Inc., 1959.

DeVoto, Bernard, *Across the Wide Missouri*. Boston: Houghton Mifflin Company, 1947.

——, *The Course of Empire*. Boston: Houghton Mifflin Company, 1952.

—— (ed.), *The Journals of Lewis and Clark*. Boston: Houghton Mifflin Company, 1953.

Dillon, Richard, *Meriwether Lewis*. New York: Coward-McCann, Inc., 1965.

182

Ferris, W. A., *Life in the Rocky Mountains*, ed. by Paul C. Phillips. Denver: Old West Publishing Co., 1940.

Garretson, Martin S., *The American Bison*. New York: New York Zoological Society, 1938.

Goetzmann, William H., *Exploration and Empire*. New York: Alfred A. Knopf, Inc., 1966.

Guthrie, A. B. Jr., *The Way West*. New York: William Sloan Associates, Inc., 1949.

————, *The Big Sky*. New York: William Sloan Associates, Inc., 1947.

Henry, Alexander (The Younger), *New Light on the Early History of the Greater Northwest*, ed. by Eliot Coues. New York: Francis P. Harper, 1897.

Innis, Harold A., *The Fur Trade in Canada*. New Haven: Yale University Press, 1962.

Irving, Washington, *Astoria*. Portland, Oregon.

————, *The Adventures of Captain Bonneville, U.S A., in the Rocky Mountains and the Far West*. Norman, Okla.: University of Oklahoma Press, 1961.

Kelly, Charles, and Morgan, Dale, *Old Greenwood*. Georgetown, Calif.: The Talisman Press, 1965.

Lahontan, Baron Louis Armande, *New Voyages to North America*, ed. by H. C. Thwaites. 2 vols. Chicago: 1905.
(Originally, "*Memoires de l'Amérique Septentrionale ou la Suite de M. le Baron Lahontan*." Amsterdam: Chez la Françoise l'Honoré et Compagnie, 1728.)

Lavender, David, *Land of Giants*. Garden City, N.Y.: Doubleday & Company, Inc., 1958.

Morgan, Lewis H., *The American Beaver and His Works*. Philadelphia: J. B. Lippincott Co., 1868.

O'Meara, Walter, *The Savage Country*. Boston : Houghton Mifflin Company, 1960.

Parkman, Francis, *The Old Régime in Canada*. 1909.
————, *La Salle and the Discovery of the Great West*. 1908.
————, *Count Frontenac and New France Under Louis XIV*. 1908.
————, *The Jesuits in North America*. 1908.
————, *Pioneers of France in the New World*. 1909.
————, *The Oregon Trail*. 1927.
    (Dates as reprinted by Little, Brown & Company, Boston.)

Rue, Leonard Lee 3d, *The World of the Beaver*. Philadelphia : J. B. Lippincott Co., 1964.
Russell, Carl P., *Firearms, Traps, and Tools of the Mountain Men*. New York : Alfred A. Knopf, Inc., 1967.
Russell, Osborne, *Journal of a Trapper*, ed. by Aubrey L. Haines. Portland, Ore. : Champoeg Press, 1955.
    (Original title, *Journal of a Trapper, or Nine Years in the Rocky Mountains, 1834-1843*.)

Sandoz, Mari, *The Beaver Men, Spearheads of Empire*. New York : Hastings House, 1964.

Wilcox, Ruth, *Mode in Hats and Headdress*. New York : Charles Scribner's Sons, 1945.

INDEX

American Fur Company, 127, 145, 149, 152–153
  Astor's share in, sold out, 167
  rendezvous of (1838), 165
  Whitman traveling with, 162, 163
American Revolution, 105
Amherst, Lord Jeffrey, 62, 71
Ashley, William, 130, 131, 132, 133, 155, 157
Astor, John Jacob, 167–168
  fur trade controlled by, 120–122, 127

Barnes, Jane, first white woman on the Columbia, 125–126
Beaujeu, Captain, 54
beaver fur, commercial importance of, to France, 10
beaver hunters, first French, 58
beaver pelts
  competition for, 120
  price of, 149, 178
  trading of, 26–27, 29, 31, 39, 43, 104
  uses for, 26
  value of, 94, 104
beaver population
  control of, 179
  reduction of, 135
  at time of white man's coming, 177–178

beavers
  abundance of, 127, 130
  American, 14, 19
  damage done by, 180
  decline in demand for, 167–168
  description of, 19–20
  eating habits of, 14
  enemies of, 19
  Eurasian, 14, 18
  legends concerning, 21–23
  mating habits of, 14
  near extermination of, 19, 153, 155, 169, 172, 177–178
  physical characteristics of, 18, 20–21
  restocking, 19, 179
  underwater breathing ability of, 17
  use of, as food, 22, 23, 40, 139
  wintering habits of, 17
  zoological classification of, 13–14
beaver trade, 30–31, 44–45, 50
  monopoly in, 30
beaver trappers, 40, 57, 59
  American, 127
  Canadian, 127
  contribution of, to winning the West, 177
  equipment needed by, 135–136
  free, 127, 130
  jobless, 173
  qualities of, 176–177

185

beaver trappers (*Cont.*)
  rivalry among, 119–120
  skills developed by, 143
  supplies needed by, 148
  winter camp of, 138
beaver trapping, 19, 58, 103, 136–137
  hazards of, 120–121
  in the Rockies, 119
  westward trend of, 119
Beckwourth, Jim, 153, 176
  autobiography of, 175
  teller of tall tales, 140–142
Bonaparte, Napoleon, 107
Bonneville, Captain Benjamin
  Louis Eulalie de, 157, 158
bourgeois, life of a, 91–92, 104
Brébeuf, Father Jean de, 42
Bridger, Jim, 130, 133, 172, 173, 176
  daughter of, massacred, 164
  operation on, by Whitman, 163
  tall tales told by, 140
Brulé, Étienne, 36, 41
buffalo, extermination of, 173
bushrangers, 44–45, 47, 63

Caen, Emery de, 37
Caen, William de, 37
California, discovery of gold in, 172
Canada
  economy of, based on fur trade, 106
  English possession of, 71, 105
  French in, 9, 30
  naming of, 28
  Scots in, 71–78
canoe fleets, 71, 74–76, 88–89
Carson, Kit, 173
Cartier, Jacques, 24, 25, 27–29, 62
Castor canadensis, 14
castoreum, uses for, 137
Castor fiber, 14
Castoridae, 14
Castoroides, beaver ancestors, 13

Chabot, Philippe de Brion, 24
Champlain, Samuel de, 30, 41
  alliance of, with Indians, 31–34, 35–37
  capture of, by Kirke, 38
  death of, 39
Charbonneau, Toussant, 110
Chardon, Francis, 168, 169
cholera epidemics, 162, 168
Chouteau, René Auguste, 57
Chouteaus, the, 109, 127
civilization, beavers' role in spread of, 9, 63
Clark, Captain William, 108, 111, 112, 113, 114, 115
codfishing, 25, 27, 29
colonies, new world, founding of, 57
  See also England
Colter, John, 115–118, 119
Columbus, 24–25
Comcomly, Chief, 123, 124, 126
Continental divide, crossing of the, 83, 119, 157
Cook, Captain James, 82
coureurs de bois, 44–45, 47, 48, 49, 59, 88

dams, beaver-built, 14, 20
de Soto, Hernando, 50
Drewyer, George, 119
Droullard, George, 114
Duluth, Sieur, 47, 88

Eels, Myra, 165
England, 9
  colonization the primary interest of, in North America, 10

felt, manufacture of, 26–27, 168
female companions, woodsmen's, 77–78, 102
Fields, Joseph, 114
Fields, Reuben, 114
Fitzpatrick, Tom, 130, 133, 145–146, 162, 163

Five Nations, League of the, 31
Forts
    Astoria, 121, 123, 127
    Atkinson, 131, 132
    Bridger, 176
    Charles, 65
    Chipewyan, 80–81
    Clarke, 168
    Clatsop, 112–113
    Crèvecœur, 51, 52
    Frontenac, 51, 52
    George, 124
    Hall, 160
    Henry, 130–131
    La Reine, 60, 61
    Mandan, 110, 111
    Manuel, 116, 118
    "Nonsense," 158
    St. Louis, 52, 54
    Union, 152–153
    Vancouver, 154, 156, 159, 164
    William, 88, 123, 125
    See also trading posts
France, 9–10, 25
    in Canada, 29
    involvement of, in American Rev-
        olution, 105
    territorial claims of, in North
        America, 33–34, 51, 52
Frobisher, Joseph, 79, 80
Frobisher, Thomas, 79
Frontenac, Count, 48, 52
fur trade, 31, 35, 44, 57
    American, 127, 130
    Astor's control of, 120
    Canada's economy based on, 106
    Canadian, 35, 37, 39
    effect of smallpox epidemic on,
        169
    English share in. *See* Hudson's
        Bay Company
    French share in, 29, 31, 35, 42
    illegal, 44
    Oregon, 159
    Rocky Mountain, 133

fur traffic, extension of, 51
fur trappers, 19, 39–40
    western migration led by, 10

gambling,   among   Indians   and
        mountain men, 147
Glass, Hugh, 131–132
Godin, Antoine, 151
gold
    discovery of, in California, 172
    importance of, to conquistadores,
        10
Grand Portage, 75, 76, 81, 87–90,
    94, 123
Gray, Captain Robert, 82, 109, 154
great migration, the, 122, 162, 170,
    172, 177
Greysolon,   Daniel.   *See*   Duluth,
        Sieur
grizzlies, 70, 131, 144, 147
Grosseilliers, Medard Chouart, Sieur
    de, 58, 64, 65

Harmon, Daniel, Canadian girl de-
        scribed by, 77
Harris, Black, 169
Hearne, Samuel, Cumberland House
        established by, 78
Henday, Anthony, 70
Henry, Alexander the Elder, 79, 105
Henry, Alexander the Younger, 100,
    103, 104, 124–125
    journal kept by, 91–97, 101, 102,
        123, 125–126
Henry, Andrew, 130, 131, 132
Hochelaga, 27, 28
homesteaders, 162, 170, 171
Hudson, Henry, 64
Hudson's   Bay   Company,   10,   58,
    64–67, 69, 78–80, 103, 109,
    119, 154, 155, 156
    Bonneville's   reports   concerning,
        158
    competition for, 80
    pelts handled by (1853–77), 178

Hudson's Bay Company (*Cont.*)
    Fort Hall sold to, 160
    "strip the country bare" policy of,
        169

Indians, 29, 35, 40, 43, 45, 55, 70,
        105
    Algonquins, 22, 31, 32, 36, 40,
        58
    Arikaras, 131
    Assiniboins, 95
    Bannocks, 145
    beaver veneration by, 21–23
    Blackfeet, 70, 114, 116–119, 121,
        130, 131, 144, 146, 153,
        159, 163
    capture of, by French, 28
    Cayugas, 32
    Cherokees, 21
    Cheyennes, 141
    Chinooks, 121–122, 123, 125
    Chippewas, 22, 47, 95
    Comanche, 156
    Crees, 69, 95
    Crows, 22, 116, 118, 140–141,
        145, 153
    Flatheads, 23, 145, 161, 164
    Fox, 47–48
    Gros Ventres, 110, 146, 151–152
    Hidatsas, 22, 109, 110
    Hurons, 31, 32, 36, 40–42, 58
    Illinois, 49
    Iroquois, 22, 31–34, 35–37, 41,
        42, 58
    Mandans, 109, 110, 119
    Mohave, 156
    Mohawks, 31–32
    Nez Percés, 113, 145, 147, 164
    Oneidas, 32
    Onondagas, 32
    Plains, 69, 110, 149
    Seminoles, 175
    Senecas, 32
    Sioux, 48
    Snake People, 61, 145
    trade with, 103–104
    Umpquas, 156
Indian wars, 173
Innis, Harold A., 177
international rivalry, beaver
    influence on, 87
Isaac Todd, 123–125

Jackson, President Andrew, 158
Jackson, ———, 133, 155
Jefferson, Thomas, 86–87
    Lewis and Clark Expedition
        ordered by, 108, 109
    Louisiana Purchase by, 106–107
Jolliet, Louis, 48–50
Journal of a Trapper (Russell),
    quote from, 143

Kearny, General Stephen, 175
Kelsey, Henry, 69–70
Kirke, Captain David, 38
kits, beaver, 14, 17

La Barre, Governor, 52–53
Laclede, Pierre, 57
Lahontan, Baron
    illegal fur-trade described by, 44
    profits estimated by, 45–46
    trading post pedlars described by,
        45
La Jemmeraye, 60
La Salle, Robert Cavalier, Sieur de,
    50–55, 106
La Vérendrye, Pierre Sieur de, 60–
    62, 63, 70, 88
    sons of, 61–62
Leavenworth, Colonel, 131, 132
Lee, the Rev. Jason, missionary,
    160–162, 170
Lewis, Meriwether, 108, 111, 112–
    115, 123
Lewis and Clark Expedition, 108,
    109–115, 116, 119, 126,
    127, 154
liquor, Indian love of, 40, 43–44,

67, 79, 91, 93–94, 145, 147, 153

Lisa, Manuel, 109, 116, 118

lodge, beaver, 20
  construction of, 14–16

Louisiana Purchase, 106–108

McDonald, John, of Garth, 80, 124, 125

McDonnell, "Big John," 80

McDougall, Duncan, 124, 126
  Astoria trading post sold by, 123

McKenzie, Daniel, 80

McKenzie, Kenneth, 153–154

McKenzie, Roderick, 80

McLoughlin, Dr. George, 154, 156

McTavish, Donald, 125, 126

McTavish, Simon, co-founder of North West Fur Company, 80, 89

Macdonnell, John, injured buffalo described by, 97

Mackay, Alexander, 83

Mackenzie, Alexander, 81, 82–86, 109, 121

Marquette, Father Jacques, 48–50

Matagorda colony, 54–56

Meek, Joe, 165
  daughter of, massacred, 164
  and the grizzly bear, 142
  petition presented to Congress by, 173
  petrified forest tale by, 140

Menzies, Archibald, 86

Mexico, war with, 171, 175

missionaries, 170
  See also Spalding, the Rev. Henry; Whitman, Dr. Marcus

missions, 42, 82

Missouri Fur Company, 131

Montcalm, Louis Joseph de, 62

Montreal, 28
  annual trading fairs at, 35, 43–44
  naming of, 27

Monts, Sieur de, beaver trade monopoly granted to, 30, 34

Moranget, nephew of La Salle, 53, 55

Mormons, 172, 176

mountain men, 10, 57, 127, 135, 153, 155, 158, 165, 169, 172, 173, 175
  battle between Indians and, 152
  gambling among, 147
  occupational disease of, 137
  tall tales told by, 118, 139–141
  women companions of, 149

nations, beaver's role in destiny of, 9, 106

Newfoundland Banks, fishermen, 25, 29

New France, 30–37, 50, 63
  Company of, 37, 38

Newhouse, Sewell, beaver-trap manufacturer, 178

New Orleans, fur-trade center, 57

North America, development of, 9, 10

Nor'westers, 80, 91, 94, 97, 103, 119

North West (Fur) Company, 81, 86, 87, 103, 109, 122–123, 154
  annual meetings of, 89–90, 94
  founding of, 80
  merger of, with Hudson's Bay Company, 154
  skins averaged per year by, 103
  wintering partners of, 90–91

Northwest Passage, search for, 25, 27, 59, 64, 69, 78

Northwest Road, 71, 75, 76, 87, 106

Ogden, Peter Skene, 155, 169

Oregon
  boundaries of, 121
  free-soil territory in, 175

Oregon Dragoons, 171

Oregon fever, 170

Oregon Trail, 122

   wagons along the, 157, 158, 170, 171, 172

overtrapping, 19, 68

   See also beaver, near extermination of

Pacific Fur Company, 120, 127

Paris, Treaty of, 62, 105, 107

partnerships, traders', 80

"pedlars," Scottish, 71, 76

pemmican, 100–101

Perrot, Nicolas, 47–48

Pierre's Hole

   battle of, 151–152, 159

   rendezvous at, 145–151, 159

Polk, James K., 171

Pond, Peter, 79, 80, 83

Pontgravé, 30–31, 34

Portugal, 25

Potts, ———, partner of John Colter, 117

Quebec, 27

   French colony at, 28–29, 30–31

Raccoon, 124

Radisson, Pierre Esprit, 58, 64–67

   trappers' hardships described, 59

rendezvous of 1832, 145–147, 149, 150–151

Roberval, Sieur de, 28–29

Rocky Mountain (Fur) Company, 145–147, 149, 152, 167

   Wyeth operating under, 159–160

Rocky Mountains, Astor expeditions in the, 122

rodents, world's largest, 13

Russell, Osborne, camping in the rain described by, 143–144

Sacajawea, 111

St. Louis Missouri Fur Company, 118

St. Louis fur-trade center, 57

Scots, in Canada, 71–78

Serra, Father Junipero, 154

Seton, Ernest Thompson, 178

Simpson, George, 154, 155

skins, average yearly take of, by Nor'westers, 103

smallpox epidemics, 58, 168

   effect of on fur trade, 169

Smith, Jedediah, 130, 131, 133, 155

   death of, 156

   Mohave Desert trapping party led by, 155–157

Spain, 9, 25

   in the Caribbean, 10

   in Florida, 105

   in Louisiana, 105

   involvement of, in American Revolution, 105

   in Mexico, 55

Spalding, Eliza, 163–164

Spalding, the Rev. Henry, missionary, 163–164

Stadacona, 27, 28

Sublette, Milton, 150–151

Sublette, William, 130, 133, 145–147, 151, 155

surveys, beaver, 179

Tabashaw, Chief, 95

Talon, ———, 59

Taylor, Colonel Zachary, 175

territorial claims in the New World, 105–106

Texas, annexation of, 171

Tonquin, loss of the, 121–122

trade items, 149–150

traders

   competition among, 78

   independent, 71, 79, 80

trading companies, St. Louis, 130

trading fairs, 35, 43, 143, 144, 169, 178

   first annual, 133

trading posts, 42
  Anticosti, 29, 39, 63
  Athabaska, 80, 81, 83
  James Bay, 67, 68
  Montreal, 35
  procedures at, 67–68
  Three Forks, 118–119
  See also Forts
trappers, beaver. *See* beaver trappers
trapping, beaver. *See* beaver trapping
trapping season, yearly, 179
traps, 19, 136, 137, 178
tree felling by beavers, 14, 18, 20

United States, role of in New World, 9

Vaca, Cabeza de, 82
Vancouver, Captain George, 82, 86, 109, 121
Vasquez, Louis, 176
Voyages from Montreal, 86

voyageurs, 71–76, 83, 87, 88, 89
  songs of the, 72–73

Walker, Joe, 158
Walker, Mary, 165
  diary kept by, 165, 166
War of 1812, 122, 127
watershed, "dead," benefited by beavers, 180–181
westward expansion, beaver, influence on, 127
Whitman, Dr. Marcus, medical missionary, 162–164, 168
Whitman, Narcissa, 163
winter camp, trappers', 138
wintering partners, 80, 89
  Northwest Company's, 90–91
Wolfe, General James, 62
women as stock-in-trade, 149
Wyeth, Nathaniel J., 159–160

XY Company, 103

York Factory, 69–70
Young, Brigham, 172